MY DOVER

JOE HARMAN

Compiled and edited by Derek Leach OBE

D.A. Leach (Riverdale Publications)
24 Riverdale River Dover CT17 0QX

Dedicated to Rosa who gave me my 'Freedom'

Published in 2001 by D.A. Leach (Riverdale Publications)
24 Riverdale, River, Dover, Kent CT17 0QX

ISBN 0 9536166 1 4

Printed in England by A.R. Adams and Sons (Printers) Ltd.
The Printing House, Dour Street, Dover, Kent CT16 1EW

*Joe being admitted as a Freeman of Dover, 28th July 1989
with Paul Watkins, Dover District Council Chairman*

iii

CONTENTS

INTRODUCTION

Why produce a book about Joe Harman? Well, a number of factors probably make him unique. He is not only a Dovorian, but one who has lived his entire life not only in the same town but in the same house in which he was born. Several generations of his family were also Dovorians. Unlike many Dovorians, Joe spent the years of the Second World War in Dover because of his reserved occupation and can tell us his personal experiences and what it was like living in Dover during those war years. In addition, Joe has always taken a keen interest both in the history of the town and in what was going on during his lifetime. This has led him to research many aspects of the town's life and to record it. Finally, he has been a keen photographer since boyhood and his photographs of Dover over his lifetime complement his written records.

Many of his memories are linked quite naturally with some of the subjects he has investigated and this book attempts to tell his own, personal story interwoven with his historical research, much of which has appeared over the past twenty years as articles in publications such as *Bygone Kent* and the *Dover Society Newsletter.*

Whilst it would be impossible to include all the little gems of information about Dover that Joe has tucked away in his head and which drop from his lips constantly, I hope that this book will satisfy not only the many people who have wanted Joe to write a book but also all those, like me, who can't learn enough about this historic town of ours.

Derek Leach

Chapter 1

MY FAMILY AND CHILDHOOD

Things start with a bang

The first aerial bomb ever to fall on Britain dropped on Dover in Taswell Street on Christmas Eve, 1914. I don't know whether that hurried my arrival into the world, but I was born four days afterwards. The bomb was dropped by a single Taube aircraft from some 5,000 feet. The pilot, Lieutenant Von Prondzynski, looked down on Dover Castle and dropped the bomb out of the cockpit by hand. It missed the castle by some 400 feet and landed in a garden next to the St. James's Church Rectory. Working in the garden up a tree was James Banks who was thrown out of the tree but was unhurt. A few windows in the rectory were smashed and a crater four feet deep appeared. Two British aeroplanes gave chase but had little hope of catching the German plane as their only armaments were said to be pistols. The pilot was given a hero's welcome in Germany and was presented with a money prize by the Kaiser for being the first German pilot to bomb Britain. Later the bomb fragments were collected, mounted on a shield and presented to King George V. The Dover Society has erected one of its Millennium plaques commemorating historic local events near the spot where the bomb fell. Although it did little damage, it did cause quite a stir – after all it was the first damage caused by a foreign enemy in Dover since the French burnt the town in 1294!

Earliest memory

My own earliest memory was a terrific bang in, I think, 1917 when a 600lb. bomb was dropped in Poulton Wood by a Zeppelin. I can still remember crawling out from under the bed which was our air raid shelter and seeing my father going out on duty. As soon as a bomb dropped all the police had to report for duty. About this time there was a violent outbreak of influenza which wiped out whole families. I caught this 'flu and I had it bad. I was taken out of bed and given a last cuddle. I said my little prayer 'Gentle Jesus meek and mild, suffer me to come to Thee' but I didn't. I recovered!

Mum with Joe in christening gown, 1915

School and diphtheria

I went to school in 1920. I should have gone to Buckland but my father managed to get me into Barton Road which was said to be a better school. In 1922 the doctor came one morning when my sister was ailing, looked down her throat and said, 'That's diphtheria.' Then he looked down my throat and said, 'He's coming along, too.' So that afternoon one of Nash's horse-drawn carriages drew up at the door and took my sister and me up the road to the isolation hospital in Noah's Ark Road – apparently it's called Noah's Ark because there used to be a Noah's Ark dairy up there. I can still hear the horse trotting up the hill. I never saw my mother and father for thirteen weeks. I was only seven. My father when he was on night shift used to come and look through the window at me but I never saw him. My sister came out after six weeks and they said I could go home, too, but they gave me a bath, then took my temperature and it was 106. It was panic stations and I was there for another six or seven weeks! I was the only one left in the hospital. It's funny the little things that stick in the memory – one day the staff said I might as well have the meals they were having. Along came this lovely shepherd's pie, but the doctor arrived, my dinner was whipped away and I never got a dinner that day! One of the funny things that came out afterwards was when one of my mates said, 'When you came out of hospital you didn't half swear!' Of course, the older lads in hospital had used all sorts of words that I picked up. My parents soon got rid of them!

There was another isolation hospital – for smallpox – up at St. Radigund's called Mount Ararat. I thought, ah, Noah's Ark and Mount Ararat, is there a link? But when I checked up, the name Mount Ararat pre-dated the isolation hospital.

Barton Road Boys' School about 1927; Joe is in the front row with a crooked tie

At school I remember getting into the next to top class. Our teacher was a bit of a weakling and she often had spells sick. When this happened we were all bunged in with another class and one teacher took the lot! I was caught talking once and the teacher, Miss Scott, said, 'When you come up to my class I'm going to sort you out.' But I got my diphtheria then and when I came out of hospital I had a gammy leg and had to be pushed round in a pushchair for a while. When I went back to school they put me in the Big Boys and so I never went into Miss Scott's top infants' class! I met her years later on the Road

Safety Committee and we became great friends, but I never reminded her of what she was going to do to me.

Of course, there was no playing field alongside the school then. That site was still occupied by St. Barnabas Church and its hall. The Tramway had a concert party and I remember them performing at St. Barnabas' church hall. Barton Road always had a good football team – I remember them beating St. Paul's 27-0! I always felt sorry for St. Paul's because they always got tanned.

I never went to grammar school. You had to buy uniform and couldn't leave school until you were sixteen. I had heard my mother talking about Dad dying and I thought, with two younger sisters, I must leave school at fourteen and get a job. So when I was asked to sit the entrance exam I refused to take it. The teacher ought to have pressed me to 'have a go, Joe'. I finished up in the top class at Barton Road at 12 and I stayed there for two years, but those of us in the top division didn't do much, we just mucked around. The headmaster was supposed to give us lessons. Those two years were wasted until I could leave at fourteen.

Fun and games
We used to play on the High Meadows behind Tower Hamlets and fly kites. In the street we whipped tops and played tip-cat – the police didn't like that – too many windows got broken. There was a history exhibition in the Stone Hall during the 1970s; I made a kite and a whip top and got people playing with them including an usher. We nearly broke one of the stained-glass windows! Just as now, some games went in and out of fashion – sometimes marbles were all the rage and then cigarette cards, then tops and kites. The shops would suddenly start selling them and the kids would want them. There used to be lots of metal bits in the gutters from horseshoes, hobnail boots and metal rims of cart wheels; we would pick them up, put them on a piece of card with a magnet underneath and the metal bits would all stand up. Recently, as an experiment I did the same thing with a magnet in the gutter and it picked up tiny iron filings from somewhere.

On November 5th we used to look out to see the local lads with their homemade 'guys' queuing up at the side gate of Grove House at the bottom of St. Radigund's Road. This was where Guy Mannering lived and he would give five bob, ie 25p, if he approved of his namesakes! I can still see their efforts perched on a four-wheel barrow. In addition to keeping rainfall records, Guy collected stuffed birds which were kept in an annexe. He lived at Grove House until he died and his widow lived there until she died. The stuffed birds ended up in Maidstone Museum. The house was then derelict for years until it was demolished to make way for the British Legion home, Charles Lister House.

I had a four-wheel barrow too and one day my barrow went out of control and crashed into the Grove House gate. I went flying through the air to collect a nasty gravel rash on both hands. Next day I went to school and the class had to write out the National Anthem. Nev King was sitting next to me and he wrote in his book, 'God save my old tom cat!' Joe, being very patriotic, objected and told Nev so in no uncertain terms! For my pains I was hauled out of my seat for talking and given two strokes of the cane on one hand. By the time I got back to my seat my hand was bleeding because of the gravel rash and Nev told the teacher, hoping to get him into trouble. The teacher asked why I hadn't held out the other hand and I said, 'That hand is even worse!'

That wasn't the only time I was in trouble at school. I remember a scripture lesson and the teacher saying that Saul died, but I knew that Saul had not died naturally. He was killed and I said so! I got a lump of chalk thrown at me for that!

Percy Harman with bowls trophy

My Dad

My dad, Percy, was born in Granville Street in 1886. I think he went to Charlton School. He worked on the trams – I think he joined when they put the trams through to River in 1905 – but then joined the police force in 1908. He and a mate, Harry Leeming, joined the police together. It was decided to have a point duty policeman at Worthington Street before there were any traffic lights and that's when they wanted more policemen and my father got in. My father was keen on first aid and lifesaving, plus ju jitsu. Bowls and cricket were favourites as football had been ruled out due to injuries. Father was proud of his pair of woods that he won in a competition in about 1911. He was promoted to sergeant in 1924 but then developed a tumour on the brain, which was inoperable in those days, and he had to retire on ill-health grounds. He just faded away and died in 1927. He was 41 and I was 12. So, I had another

Funeral procession of Percy Harman, 8th May 1927

ride in one of Mr Nash's carriages but this time to my father's funeral. This could have been one of the last horse-drawn funerals because Mr Nash closed his stables in 1927.

My Mother
My mother was Alice Whitehead and she was born in St. Mary-in-the-Marsh, so that's why I've got links with Romney Marsh. She came to Dover where she had a cousin and her uncle was on the trams. She got a job in service with a Doctor Ruby who had a house on the seafront in Waterloo Mansions. Mum slept in an attic under the roof. Soon after she started work there she found a gold sovereign on the stairs and she asked Cook what she should do about it. It was a test of my mother's honesty by the lady of the house! Cook said that she would fix it and she did, by nailing the sovereign on to the stairs!

Mum and Dad
Mum and Dad married in 1913. I was born in 1914 and my sisters in 1917 and 1921. My father had already bought a house at 1, Pioneer Road but Mother would not move in because she did not want to live next door to a pub, the *Gate Inn*! So he had to get somewhere else and they moved into the home of Sergeant Maxted who had recently died. He lived at 16, St. Radigund's Road (later renumbered 23) which was built in 1869 and is where I still live. Father rented this house and hoped to buy it but the owner died and left it to his wife in trust as long as she lived. So Father could never buy it. Eventually, the old lady died when my father was dying. It came on the market and he bought it for £350, but then Mother had the problem of paying off the Oddfellows' mortgage. They reduced the repayments as far as they could. Anyway, there was a bit of rent coming in from the Pioneer Road property, but fortunately the tenant died and we sold the house and cleared our mortgage. Mother was left with us three kids. My father was given a little job when he had to retire of collecting money off errant husbands: the man came one day and paid the money in; then the wife came a day or two later and collected it. When Dad died, Mother carried it on for a bit. The police used to give her little escort jobs which brought in a little bit, but money was tight. We got an allowance from the Widows and

Wedding photograph of Alice Whitehead and Percy Harman, October 1913

Joe with Mum and Dad and sister Trudie

Orphans Fund that helped a little, too. Then the Borough Council who employed the Town Police paid a pension but somebody tripped up and overpaid Mother and she had to pay it back, which made things very dodgy, but we did manage to get by. So, one way and another I had to grow up a bit quick.

My mother died from kidney failure in 1940 when she was 52. Both my parents might have been saved today by operations. My oldest sister, Trudie, was already married when Mum died. Her husband was called up and she came to live with us, but Trudie finished up in New Romney with my grandmother. My other sister, Joyce, was called up to work in a Glaxo factory outside London but she didn't like it so, she thought she would join the Land Army, but the officials said she had applied for industry and my sister replied, 'Well, isn't agriculture an industry?' She enjoyed the Land Army.

Mother and Joyce outside 23 St. Radigund's Road with the iron railings which were removed in 1942

Chapter 2

THE TOWN POLICE FORCE 1836-1943

Since both my father and grandfather were policemen in Dover, researching the history of the Dover Police Force was an obvious interest for me later in life. Sadly my father died when I was twelve and my grandfather in 1916 when I was one and so I was not able to glean much information in that direction, but I have to thank my Dad's old comrades for their help.

I examined the Watch Committee minutes for Dover which contain a lot of information about the early days of the Dover Police Force. I was pleased to note in the minutes that there was a George Harman the younger recruited in 1837, but after he had been discovered in a public house a couple of times the Committee accepted his resignation. The 1841 Census shows him as a miller following in his father George's footsteps.

Watchmen

Prior to 1836 the Paving Commission was responsible for providing the Watch. Most of these were old men who were paid 15/- a week in winter and 10/6d. in summer. In 1808 we find that, in order to keep the watchmen to their duties, they were paid two weeks in arrears. In 1809 they were to be compensated for the increased price of candles at the end of the year, and in 1810 'Watchmen as have not rattles to be provided with them'. Up to 1818 a tower in Townwall Street (roughly on the site of the present *Britannia Inn*) was used by the 'Constable of ye night to keep ye Watchmen to their duties'. Watchboxes were provided in various parts of the town, and it was the delight of the local lads to turn the box over when the old chap was inside. In 1831 the Paving Commissioners decided to appoint a Chief Constable and two assistants, although the Night Constable was to continue with nine Watchmen. The Chief and his assistants were to be on duty from 7 am until 10 pm. The Chief Constable's salary was £50 per annum plus £6 for uniform and the assistants received £35 plus uniform of an inferior quality valued at £5. They had many duties including being present when

George Harman 1846-1916, Joe's grandfather, fond of rabbit shooting

passengers were embarking and disembarking from the Channel Packets, supervising the scavenging and watering of the streets, reporting nuisances and dealing with vagrants, to see that the provisions of Acts of Parliament were carried out, and to obey the orders of the Justices.

On January 20th 1836 three sergeants and twelve constables went on duty taking their orders from the newly formed Watch Committee. Richard Lushington Crosoer, who had been Chief, was now a PC. A month later Henry Crosoer was appointed Inspector, and in March 1839 Superintendent Correll took charge. By that time there were fifteen constables, but by 1841 the numbers had dropped to twelve, due to economy measures. In 1844 there was the murder of PC Couchman at Charlton but this did not lead to an increase in manpower until 1851. By 1846 Correll had resigned and Sergeant Laker had been promoted but in 1850 he was forced to resign after attempting 'self destruction'; John Rofe from Walsall was appointed, but in a year he had returned to that town to take over a commercial inn. John Coram, who had been second choice, and came from the Fleet Street station, replaced him and continued until 1872 when another London man, Thomas Sanders, took over up to 1901.

A policeman's lot was not a happy one
To return to the early days of the Force we find that the Metropolitan Force was consulted about uniforms and rules for the new police. Discipline was enforced by suspension, reduction in wages and fines. Later, when classes were created, they were able to put them down a grade. The greatest offence seems to have been drinking on duty and with the number of inns and alehouses it was difficult to avoid walking into one of them. A rule was made that it would mean instant dismissal if found drinking on duty, but this was later rescinded due to shortage of men. They did get round it by allowing a good man to re-apply. Hot coffee was taken out to the night men during the winter months to try to alleviate

Dover Police about 1895, George Harman is one of the sergeants

the situation. Supernumerary Police were recruited to fill the gaps and also for elections at 5/- a day. There are lists of these; sometimes 50 and at others 100. In 1872 there was a riot after the declaration of the Poll and this caused the resignation of John Coram who was getting past it anyway. They tried to convict some of the troublemakers but they could not find witnesses as there was a conspiracy of silence. There was also the annual Easter Review of the Volunteers which caused problems and police were drawn from other Forces including Rochester, Brighton, Margate, Maidstone and Gravesend; the railway companies gave them free passes.

In June 1837 an instruction was given, that from this night, officers were to call 'Patrole' at the distance of every 20 yards on their respective beats. In February 1842 the order was changed to calling every five minutes. Street lighting was very poor and non-existent during summer months, or at the time of the full moon. The Superintendent did point out that on one cloudy night in April 1853 it was impossible to police, as people were walking into each other. No doubt the smugglers and other miscreants preferred the darkness, and also liked to know the whereabouts of the Police. In 1905 we notice that six dozen Wood Milne Silent Rubber Heels had been purchased.

Police Officers were not allowed to smoke on duty or to carry umbrellas and Sergeants were not permitted to drink with the men in a public house. In 1868 rules were reprinted: 'PCs shall not appear in plain clothes when off duty without permission of the Superintendent, or leave the borough. If, when on duty they are found engaged in conversation with female servants, or other women, they will be severely punished.' They were not to make a practice of calling people early unless a special bell had been provided. In more recent times it was usual for one of the night constables to give a couple of taps on a drain-pipe, and call back to receive a steaming hot cup of tea in the bakehouse. The Superintendent was to take care that new straw, with a clean bed tick and bedding, be provided in each cell once at least every three months.

Squaddies
Dover, being a garrison town, had odd bouts of trouble with the troops as a minute of 29th May 1862 states: 'Savage and unprovoked attack on Police by Military'. There was trouble in Snargate Street when the Grand Shaft Guard was turned out with both police and civilians being detained. In 1860 The First Company of Cinque Port Volunteers were allowed to deposit their carbines in the Police Station if racks were provided and maintained. There was also need for extra policing when royalty passed through the port, and sometimes there was no prior notice of the event. In 1855 they received two days extra pay after the success of the visit of the Emperor and Empress of France. Mention is made of the expense of barriers to keep the peace when the Shah of Persia visited this country in May 1873.

Uniforms and equipment
I should mention something about uniforms and equipment. In 1836 this included blue coats with embroidered collars; blue dress trousers; blue undress trousers; greatcoats; embroidered collar badge; stocks and clasps; button brushes and sticks; rattles; armlets; belts; boots; lanthorns; and staves. Hats were replaced with helmets in 1869, and rattles by whistles in 1872. In 1874 Sergeants had to have chevrons; pocket books were first mentioned in 1909.

There were items on staves or truncheons and in August 1866 a decision was made to increase the number of staves to 200, that is, a further 175, to be numbered and lettered

V.R. A book called 'The Policeman's Lot' by Mervyn Mitton has illustrations of three Dover truncheons and one could be part of this batch. In January 1868 '1,000 staves for Special Constables were to be made of billets of ash split, and also armlets.' These staves worked out at 4/4d. This would appear to be a reaction to the Fenian Riots in 1867. In 1898 Captain Parry, HM Inspector, commented on the large size of truncheons, and so the Superintendent was told to have them 'turned down', and I presume that the PCs had to borrow from the Specials while theirs were reduced in girth on the lathe. My father was lucky after he split his trying to kill a rat, and was able to swap with a Special Constable. The police were also the Fire Brigade with the Superintendent as the Captain. In 1880 the police were excused parading before the monthly meeting of the Watch Committee due to a fire the night before.

Scutt and Faith

I have managed to compile a card index of all members of the Force, and I thought a couple might be of interest. John Scutt who joined in 1845 was given paid leave in August 1849 because he had lost his wife and four children in one week during a cholera epidemic. Dover was fortunate to have few cases, and in thanksgiving money was raised to set up the Royal Victoria Hospital. Scutt seems to have fallen foul of the local Justices when giving evidence in Court, as he was suspended, demoted and finally dismissed by them in 1861. He took the blame when a publican was convicted in 1859, as he should have warned the landlord that prostitutes were assembling in his house. In 1855 he did attempt to leave Dover by applying for the post of Inspector at Ashford. John Faith retired in 1875 after 24 years service and the Minutes read: 'At the request of the Force, the Mayor presents John Faith with a silver tobacco box, some plate, and a portrait of himself subscribed by the Force.'

Duties, kids and dogs

In 1841 there was a list of nine beats to be covered at night, and this must have presented some difficulty as the Force had been reduced to 12 PCs. During the day someone had to be on duty at the harbour, and also to keep the narrow streets clear of obstructions including vagrants and drunks. Later when the railway came they had to deal with touters for the hotels and also fly drivers. I suppose they had to shrug their shoulders, and carry out the last order. There was, of course, attendance at the local court and trips to Maidstone Assizes. Periodically there were complaints of youngsters throwing stones and one favourite target was the china insulators on the telegraph poles. Tip-cat was another pastime frowned on, and it was reported fifty 'cats' had been confiscated. I suppose the lads made some more, as we did in our younger days, and kept a weather eye open for the copper. Catapults were another problem, and one PC was off sick due to an injury from this cause.

A minute of November 1860 is one I like: 'Instructions are given to the Force to use their discretion with regard to the trundling of hoops by children, but not to prevent it unnecessarily, and to tell them that The Parade was the most convenient place for the purpose.' Stray dogs were another thing to deal with, and I can remember my father carrying a dogline coiled up like a small clothes line. From 1866 an officer was appointed as Markets' Inspector, and this continued at least until 1915. From 1876 a policeman was to live in the old Toll Gate House opposite the *Three Cups*. It would seem that it was his job to collect Coal Dues for the Corporation, when coal could arrive by train at Kearsney instead of by boat.

Inspections and unions

After the passing of the Police Act of 1856 certain changes took place, including the annual visit by HM Inspector of Constabulary who had to give a report on efficiency. There was a grant of 25% towards the cost of Watching the town, and it was not payable unless a certificate was issued. The first report was not very good, especially in regard to numbers and lengths of beats and so the grant was withheld until extra police were employed. This happened on a number of occasions up to 1914. Reading between the lines the police had become disgruntled over wages and conditions and the Police Union was formed in 1919. My father was a member; I remember seeing his badge and also the notice from the Government which led to the forming of the Police Federation, and he did himself speak at a meeting in the Albert Hall. He was Secretary of the Constables Branch Board from October 1920, and its Chairman when he resigned on promotion to Sergeant in 1924.

In 1915 my father and PC Roberts gave artificial respiration to a crew member from a drifter who had fallen into the dock. They had worked on him for some time and the doctor was prepared to pronounce life extinct, but Father

Percy Harman, 1925

Dover Police 1920

11

decided to carry on and they were successful in reviving him. My father was sorry to hear that six months later the sailor's boat was mined in the Straits and he did not survive. Dad might have seen the end of the Dover Force in 1943 but his fatal illness in 1927 was the end of his career.

Women of the night
There were strict rules about policemen talking to 'women of the night' or 'nymphs of the pavement' as they were sometimes called. On one occasion the Inspector spotted my father on duty talking to a woman and jumped to the wrong conclusion! It was my mother. She was not amused.

Police stations
In 1881 the Police Station was moved to the Maison Dieu, where they used some of the cells from the former prison which had been there since 1834. The doorway to the right of the main steps leads down into this area which has been flooded at times, as has the Chief Constable's office. There were Chief Constables from 1901. In 1940 the police moved into the present building in Ladywell which was bombed two months later, and water poured in from the river to flood the Control Room. H.A. Saddleton was Acting Chief Constable until the end of the Dover Police Force at midnight on March 31st 1943.

Chapter 3

SCOUTS AND GUIDES

I joined the Scouts when I was ten in 1925. There was a boy down the road in the Charlton Scouts – the oldest troop in Dover. They were formed in 1907 before Baden-Powell launched the Scout Movement. The log book from those days made fascinating reading. They ran a fête in Pencester Gardens and things like that. You had to be 11 to join and when I was asked how old I was I whispered, 'Nearly' but said quite loud '11' and I got in! They had a band – I didn't play but I carried the colours when we marched. There was always a very enjoyable Whitsun camp at Old Park.

Joe, 1st Dover Charlton Scouts, 1926

Joe, Rover Scout, 1934

Eventually I was Cub Master and Scout Master. When I started work it was difficult to fit in with my shifts, but the lads stuck by me and turned up on different nights of the week to suit my shifts. One evening when I knew I was going to be late for the meeting, I set up a game to keep them going, a treasure hunt of some sort, but it all went haywire when I was told I had to work all that evening! When I went on the buses in 1937 I couldn't do it any more because of the difficult shifts.

I got very hot under the collar at times about various changes and was very incensed in about 1948 when Major Arbuthnot, the prospective Conservative candidate for Parliament, was appointed as District Commissioner. My view was that he should resign if he were elected M.P. The County Commissioner called a meeting and it was suggested that we could have two Labour Assistant Commissioners to balance the political parties! I insisted that politics should be kept out of the Scout Movement and was then interviewed by people from Scout H.Q. in London. Eventually, we had a different Commissioner appointed.

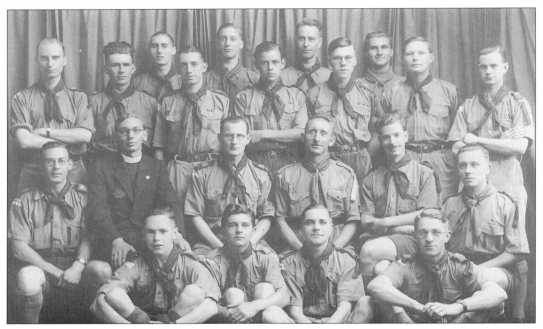

15th Dover (St. Andrew's) Rovers – Joe second from left standing

Hell fire cottage

In 1941 I met Arthur Young, a member of my old Scout troop and he said, 'You ought to come out to the Guide Cottage. We have some fun up there!' I strolled out to the cottage the next Thursday and was accepted as one of the gang. Beyond what is now the Elms Vale recreation ground, near where the road forks, on the right on the side of a hill is a ruined cottage – just a few flint walls – but the Guides had it on a peppercorn rent from about 1935 and used it regularly.

The local Girl Guides had the vision of a place to meet out in the country. Trix Rogers managed to arrange a lease of this farm cottage with a local landowner, Mr Murray Lawes, and a number of people including fathers and brothers helped to lick it into shape. It was used quite often but then the war came and most of the youngsters were evacuated to Wales. However, there still remained a small nucleus of people working on essential services in Dover.

In January 1941 Baden-Powell died in Kenya, and it was agreed to hold a Memorial Service at the cottage. On 18th January a motley crowd trooped out to the cottage in the snow. It was then decided to have further meetings, and to encourage more Service people

Ruins of The Cottage in 1986 with Harry and Kitty Greenland (nee Dorken), Rosa and Joe

to join in. Sunday meetings were arranged fortnightly and also a meeting on the first Thursday in the month. On my first visit on 6th March I was accepted as one from the 1st Dovers. On returning home I was very soon rummaging in the drawer for my shirt and shorts plus neckerchief, for the following Sunday afternoon. A Naval man, 'Sticky'

Guide Cottage after restoration

15

Kath Scarborough (nee Godfrey) with the Cottage Visitors' Book, 1986 at a display in the old Dover Museum

(H.T. Wickham) from Dartford, and Kath Godfrey from the Telephone Exchange were the prime movers in the outfit.

Naturally we had a good campfire sing-song around a roaring log fire, helped by steaming mugs of cocoa. Scottish Dancing was introduced by two Royal Marines who had been serving in the Orkneys: the Eightsome Reel, Petronella, Strip the Willow and the Dashing White Sergeant, although when I was on the floor there was the suggestion of dashing white elephants!

The Rangers and Rovers had their own activities, with the former calling themselves the 'Dover Patrol'. Some of the evacuees returned to Dover, and a District Scout Group was formed, together with a Guide Company run by members of the Cottage Unit. It was then that I started Badge examining for the Guides and am still allowed to continue this after fifty years. The Rovers had been meeting in various places including Old St James's

Round the log fire at The Cottage, January 1941,
Harry Greenland, Rosa Cloke, Kath Godfrey and Claud Wilson

16

Bomb-damaged old St James's Church soon after the Rovers ceased to meet there

Church tower and luckily had moved up to the cottage by the time the tower received a direct hit. During the War we used to walk to the cottage but one night we decided to go to Eaves Hall and what did Jerry do? He decided to bomb Clarendon and we spent more time on the floor than anything else. When the bombing stopped we picked ourselves off the floor, mopped up the spilt cocoa and decided to trek out to the cottage the next month.

The Bulletin
Numbers grew from all ranks of the Services thanks to notices in Forces canteens and some of our members assisting in them including Rosa, who helped at the Biggin Hall Canteen and whom I later married. The cottage was blessed with a well, and the winding gear was improved. Fuel was obtained from a wood nearby and food was brought out by the girls with assistance from their mothers, supplemented by a small ration. Local parsons, Army and Navy Padres came out to take Sunday Services and joined in the activities afterwards. Local lads were being called up, and others were being posted, and so at the instigation of 'Sticky' we decided to produce a Bulletin for circulation far and wide. Reports of our doings were included with letters which started to come in from various parts of the globe. At first they came from Gibraltar, South Africa and Australia, but later from North Africa, Normandy and Russia. The Bulletin was headed similarly to Baden-Powell's 'Mafeking Mail': 'Published monthly, shells and other circumstances permitting'. We were fortunate to have someone in an office who could get it duplicated, and thanks to a very efficient secretary these were mailed to their destinations and we produced over fifty editions. I can remember drafting bits for it with the 'whoompf' of bombs and shells going on. It carried on for 52 months until the War ended. During the War Winston Churchill was made Lord Warden; we sent him congratulations and had a reply.

Two very keen members, Hank and Cully, used to walk in some eight miles from Nonington to be with us. They were in the Tank Corps and later I had a letter from Italy which was published in the Bulletin. They mentioned that one night they were about to bed down near a church. Then they thought it would be a good idea to sleep down in its stokehold. It smelt a little musty, but when they woke they were not alone, as there were coffins on shelves all around them!

One day the Rangers had been using their growing knowledge of semaphore to send messages to the Rovers on the other side of the valley, when a man walking up the road joined in. The Rovers were very mystified until they received the message 'Tea's Up' and discovered that the interloper was an ex-Navy signals rating who was pleased to use his old skills.

We went out to the cottage in all weathers, and one day we realised the well had frozen up. Not to be denied our mugs of cocoa we filled the dixie with shovels of snow and waited for it to melt before adding more. Some wag asked what the shovel was last used for and I said that I had used it to remove cowpats off the hockey pitch. One or two looked a bit sick! I was lucky to get some film to record our various events, including Visitors' Day, when Mums and Dads came along, and also the almshouse folk, who had been quartered in an old mansion up the road.

Lady Baden-Powell

Our great event was the visit of Lady Baden-Powell on Sunday 18th October 1942. Her visit included presenting a Silver Cross to Joyce Fagg, a Dover Guide who had taken great risks to render first aid during a bout of shelling. The County Commissioner brought our guest by car, but she was ambushed at the boundary to be towed the last two hundred yards to save petrol. Two young Scouts were detailed to attach the ropes, with myself checking the knots. To my horror I realised that one of the lads had not allowed enough rope for his round turn and two half-hitches and so I re-tied it as I would not have lived it down if one of the teams of Rovers had fallen flat on their faces. Then I looked at my hands and realised I had collected some very black grease from the axle. Going up the field I kept wiping my hands on the grass as I knew I would be shaking hands shortly with the Chief Guide. Some years later I was doing a St John's duty at a Guide rally at the Duke of York's School, when Lady Baden-Powell stopped to speak to me. When I mentioned the cottage she remembered it well and wanted to know if we had kept in contact; then someone had a fit and I had to go and attend to her.

Lady Baden-Powell at The Cottage, 18th October, 1942 with District Commissioner Miss Elnor and Kath Godfrey in the background

On yer bike Joe

We used to make our way home as a crowd; gradually people dropped off as they reached home and I was left walking with a very nice girl, a Ranger, Rosa Cloke, who I found lived further up my road. Rosa said that she would go out on her bike the following week. Well, what did Joe have to do? He had to get a bike! I happened to speak to my bus inspector, Jack Graves, and he said, 'My boy's been called-up, he won't need his bike. You can have it for a quid.' Rosa always laughed about that – Joe had a bike within 24 hours! Our courting was done in the blackout and so nobody knew about it for a while. One mate of mine said that he had heard me out with a bird the previous night and I was seen cycling over Tower Hamlets with a girl. I replied that I went out with one girl but always came back with six!

Frights

We were very lucky one night as we came down the valley singing at the top of our voices in the moonlight. I was ahead and suddenly saw a glint of cold steel and I shouted 'stop' and fortunately the girls obeyed orders. There was a line of soldiers across the road with fixed bayonets; apparently they thought we were Nazi paratroops. Identity cards were brought out and we were allowed to proceed on our way, but I often wondered if their rifles were loaded.

  We had a concert party which helped to entertain the 'cave-dwellers' in the shelters in Dover. The night after the bombing of the East Kent Garage they were due at the East Cliff Caves. Rosa and her pal Jean were making their way along the seafront with some trepidation when large lumps of chalk started to roll down on to the road and they raced to the shelter in time for the entertainment.

  The cottage had a narrow escape when a Halifax bomber returning from a mission crashed in a field nearby. I went out on my cycle to check and met up with the Rev. Galpin, a local vicar, who had taken some of our services. As we talked we realised we were between two lots of firing as our gunners were just getting the measure of the 'doodle-bugs' over Capel and shelling had started in Dover.

Hanky panky?

At one time I was called to account by the District Commissioner due to some garbled accounts of what we got up to at the cottage. I was able to reassure him that nothing untoward happened. Nevertheless, ten marriages took place between Guides and Scouts who had met through the cottage. One was my own to Rosa in 1945. The cottage members' present to us was a lovely

The gang outside The Cottage during the War

brass rose bowl with matching vases, brought back from India by Claud Wilson, who had been associated with cottage activities from the outset and who was by now flying with the RAF. Sadly, on his next flight from the Far East, bringing back prisoners of war, he crashed at Benghazi.

We did try to keep the cottage going after the war but even then vandals were a problem. One day, for instance, we found the Elsan closet thrown down the well. Eventually the farmer claimed the cottage back, saying that she needed it to house German POWs who were working for her.

Reunions

A reunion was held at the cottage in 1947 with some camping in the field nearby. The second reunion was not held until 1963 at Eaves Hall with no outside noises-off and the floor only rocking from Highland Dancing. We had a wonderful meal, provided by the 'Cottage Catering Corps' and plenty of chatter about old times. After that there were several get-togethers at our house in St. Radigund's Road. While Rosa was in Kearsney Manor Nursing Home we had an event there, but Rosa was not well enough to join in. I took two of her old pals up to her room; even though she was facing the wall, Rosa knew them by name. I am still in contact with those that remain, now scattered and getting fewer as the years pass.

Cinema and theatre

When I was a teenager I went to the cinema quite a bit. I remember going to the old Regent – where the T.A. Drill Hall is now in London Road – and sitting in the front row getting a crick in my neck. I went to the King's Hall Cinema in Biggin Street and occasionally to the Hippodrome Theatre in Snargate Street to see the DODS (Dover Amateur Operatic and Dramatic Society) productions. I did not know it at the time, but I must have watched Rosa in *Rose Marie* because DODS were short of dancers and got some Guides involved in a totem pole dance.

The Guides used to put on pantomimes. I got roped in once by Miss Elnor, the Vicar of St. Mary's daughter, to work the lights in the gallery when I was in the Rover Scouts. I was in the Buckland Rovers who were a lively crowd – we all trouped down to the photographers one Sunday morning in uniform and had a lovely group picture taken.

I was Deep Sea Scout Liaison Officer during the War to keep in touch with Scouts who had gone into the Navy. After the War *HMS Salisbury* got in touch with me and asked if I could organise something for the lads when they came ashore. I got in touch with Reg Thomas of the 15th Dover Buckland Troop who put on a canoeing demonstration. Some of the girls who came to the cottage were Sea Rangers.

Badges

During and after the War I had the job of badge examiner for the Guides and I'm still doing it – for First Aid, Map Reading, Path-finding. One of the badges was for detailed local knowledge – where telephone boxes were and so on. Later its title was changed to 'Intimate Knowledge of the Locality.' In Rosa's list of badge examiners it was abbreviated to 'Intimate Knowledge – Joe Harman'! That was pretty good for the Guide Movement. You have to laugh! I tested the Scouts for a similar badge and they needed to know the position of all public telephone boxes. As I had to cover the whole town I wrote to the G.P.O. for a list but was told this information was not available to the public. I mentioned this to Stan Wells of the *Dover Express* and the story was soon on the front page of the *News Chronicle*. I got my list!

Chapter 4

TRAM CONDUCTOR

In March 1929 I was off sick from school with 'flu when Harry Leeming said that there was a job going on the trams as a conductor, report Monday morning. That's how as a lad of 14 I started work with a week learning the ropes with another conductor, Nobby Clark, who was my best man eventually. Then I was on the road on my own.

Many Old Dovorians still speak about the days when trams were a very cheap form of transport. The fare for a workman before 8.30 a.m. was one old halfpenny from Buckland to the Pier, and one old penny at the end of 1936. During the day it was possible to travel from the centre of the town to River for less than our present penny.

Tramway route
Starting from the Buckland Tram Shed at Buckland Bridge, which is still standing (Hollis' Garage) the route of the tramway went down the London Road and High Street to the Town Hall and then through Biggin Street, Cannon Street, Market Square and Bench Street. The top of Snargate Street was too narrow and so we took the next turning (Northampton Street) swinging back to Snargate Street near the Masonic Hall and on down to the Railway Packet Yard and left into the Dock area via Strond Street to the Crosswall, passing the old Harbour Station. The Maxton route started at the Orange Tree and went down the Folkestone Road to Worthington Street to connect with the main line. The River extension left the main road at the present traffic lights on Crabble Hill, then on to the Crabble Athletic Ground where it ran on sleeper tracks along Lewisham Road to the present bus terminus.

The beginning
In November 1895 the Dover Town Council decided to apply for an Order to enable them to run trams in the Borough. This would not have been feasible a few years earlier as the main street was very narrow from the Town Hall to the Market Square. About 1893 the frontages in Biggin Street and Cannon Street were set back, and by looking up you can see the dates when most of the properties were rebuilt. The main line from the Crosswall to Buckland was completed in time for the grand opening on the 6th September 1897 and by December 11th the Maxton route was operational. As the Buckland Tram Depot had not been completed the trams

Tramcar 23 with Alf Binge driving

World War I tram conductresses

were assembled on land which is now Balfour Road, and then shunted on to the main line at Cherry Tree Avenue. The first tram, a number 3, was driven by the Mayor over the mainline section. During the First World War women were recruited as tram conductresses.

Some time ago I was lucky enough to locate some old half plate glass negatives in a friend's garden shed. They must have been there for at least thirty years but were still in a reasonable condition. With the help of Ray Warner it was possible to get some prints and the results were surprising. The great find was a picture of number 3 in a stripped down condition at Maxton and also one of it refurbished. Apparently in 1916 there had been a collision in thick fog on single track and the old veteran of 1897 was parked on the spare track at Buckland in the hopes of repair after the War. These pictures seem to date from the early 1920s, and we know that Jim Pollard had done some very good work with limited facilities to bring cars back into service. The Maxton Depot was small

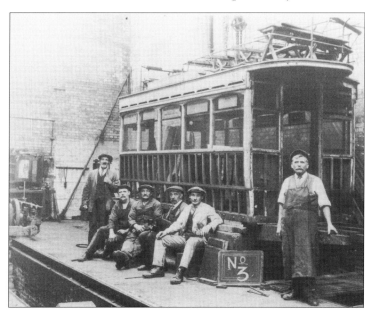

Tramcar 3 stripped down in Maxton Depot

with two tracks and room for six cars in all. The repair staff had the use of only a small portion of the shed and carried out some very good work under difficult conditions.

At the start of 1897 there were ten cars and two of these were trailers, but we know that number 10 had been motorised in 1898. Plans were afoot in the early 1900s by a private syndicate for a tramway extension to River with a possible continuation through the Alkham Valley to Folkestone. However the Corporation took over these powers in 1904 partly to relieve unemployment, and also there had been an extension of the borough boundaries in that direction in that year. On the 2nd October 1905 the River route was opened.

Tramcar 3 refurbished and ready for the road.

The River service

When I started work as a conductor, my first job was to learn how to put the trolley on the right wire and to lash the trolley pole rope for quick release. It was snowing at the time,

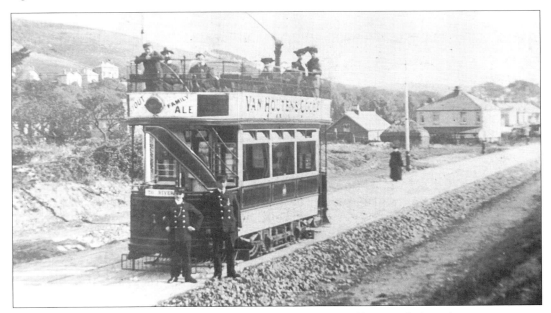

Tram 17 at the new terminus at River, October 1905; driver was Joe's uncle

and it was a great incentive to get the wheel in position quickly when particles of ice were hitting your face while gazing upwards. Most of the trams were open top at this time but three spare tops had been bought from a Birmingham undertaking and fitted to the newer cars – numbers 25, 26 and 27. In 1930 five second-hand cars with covered tops were bought from the same area, and this improved conditions for passengers and staff. One real problem was the low railway bridge on the chute leading down to River. This meant no covered cars on this route, and as every third car was on the River service it caused problems in bad weather. There were a few brave souls who still continued to ride on top to get the fresh air.

After about three years I was promoted to the River service which had the best drivers because of the safety problems going down the Crabble Chute. River was really still a village and we 'River men' were accepted as part of the community. I used to know all the girls who got on the trams. Some of the drivers would let the conductors drive the tram along the Lewisham Road sleeper track at night when there was nobody about and no

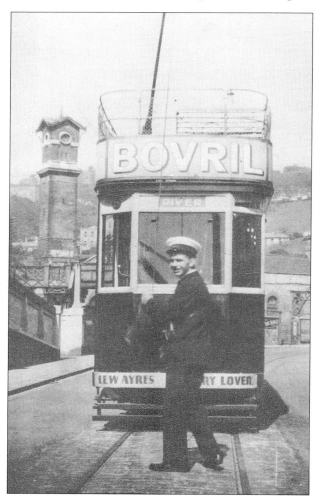

Conductor Joe at the Crosswall Terminus in the Pier District, 1935

passengers. One foggy night I had to get on the front of the tram to keep watch as there was a cow on the line! On another day we were going along the sleeper track when we stopped suddenly and the driver shot up the stairs to two boys who had been tadpoling; unfortunately, they had upset the jam jars all over him standing below!

One of the drivers, Vic, got promoted to the River route in the last days of the trams and asked me to take his photograph. So I thought I would play a joke on him; I put a large 'L' plate on the back of the tram so that when it reached River and the driver went to the other end to drive back I would take the photo complete with the 'L' plate. As I took it I looked round and Alderman Russell was coming along – in those days you were scared stiff of Councillors because the Town owned the trams. Fortunately, he always walked along with his head down and he didn't see the 'L' plate! I showed the photo to everybody but Vic didn't want one! The manager had one on his desk right till the end.

Problems at The Pier

I well remember one day when a railway employee was the only occupant of the top deck going down Snargate Street. Suddenly there was a burst of strong language from above, and on climbing the stairs I discovered that a seagull had deposited a 'fried egg' on his lap. I learnt a few new words as I endeavoured to clean things up. Another memory was a very windy day at the Crosswall Terminus while struggling to get the trolley head to mate with the wire. My uniform hat was whisked away and went bowling towards the dockside. I left the pole to its own devices, and went in pursuit, but I lost the race. I was loaned a sou'wester by the landlord of the Hotel de Paris, and on my next trip was presented with my cap which had been retrieved by a boatman and duly put into an oven to dry. As you may guess my size 7 was now 6⅜, but I was saved from further ribbing by the ticket checker bringing a spare hat from home with a bootlace attached to make sure I did not repeat the performance!

One problem in the early days was the Pier Terminus which was beyond the railway in Clarence Place. At the moment there is just one pub, *The Cinque Ports*, in this street to remind us of the old Pier District. From reports in the *Dover Express* it would seem that after about two months it became necessary to give up going over the level crossing as trams became trapped due to shunting of trains, and the consequent disruption of timetables. However, the track was not taken up until 1912 and was then used to create the 'Spur' at New Bridge to enable extra trams to be parked when military bands were performing at the Granville Gardens. In the years before the 1914-18 War there were plans to build a viaduct over the railway tracks with the intention of taking the trams over to the entrance to the Marine Station. The war intervened and the viaduct was not built until 1922 but the trams never took that route. In 1925 a footbridge was constructed at the Crosswall to enable workers and visitors to the Western Beach avoid waiting at the level crossing.

Clangers!

There was a special arrangement to ensure a connection at Worthington Street between main line and Maxton Services. The tram from Maxton would activate a red light at

Tram and trailer at the Pencester Road/Worthington Street junction

Worthington Street as it passed a point near the Priory Station, and so the other cars waited to transfer passengers. I remember one occasion when a passenger from Buckland wanted to catch a certain train, and as we reached the top of Pencester Road I saw the Maxton car departing. I jumped off and blew a long blast on my whistle and stopped the Maxton car, but looking round I saw my own tram heading down the street having mistaken my whistle blast as a signal to proceed. I started to run in pursuit but thanks to a cyclist's intervention I was able to catch up on the waiting car in the Market Square.

I nearly came a cropper once when I was almost crushed between two trams. The drivers used to change trams at Buckland by stepping off one onto the other whilst both were still moving. Silly old Joe tried to follow suit, but I missed the other tram platform and was whirled round three times in the air. I was lucky not to have my chest crushed by the two trams and my tin ticket box, but I managed to put the tin above my head and I was still standing unscathed when the trams finished passing each other! We couldn't report the accident because I shouldn't have done it and neither should the drivers!

Salvation Army accident
In about 1929, just before Christmas, the Salvation Army were singing carols in a circle near the former St. Bartholomew's Church. Our tram was standing at the stopping place, facing down town near the top of Bridge Street. A car careered up the street narrowly missing the tram and ploughed into the carol singers. My mate shouted through the passenger section to say that we would call the police. We went flat out down the High Street to stop outside the old Police Station, and Vic Tutt nipped down the passageway to inform the Station Sergeant. We later discovered that the car driver was using a method of starting his vehicle not to be recommended. He had jacked-up the back wheel, put it in gear and set the throttle. He spun the back wheel and the engine burst into life and rocked off the jack and the car took off. Sadly, one of the Salvation Army lasses was killed.

While I was doing some maintenance on my Clyno in the yard one day in 1936, an emergency call came through from the Train Ferry Dock contractors. Steve Freeman said, 'Jump aboard, as I may not be able to find Fred, and you do have your First Aid Certificate.' Fred was out shopping, and we proceeded down town nearly coming to grief when a young lady decided to run across the road at St. Mary's Church. Fortunately the wood blocks were not too greasy that morning, and we managed to stop. We went on to the Crosswall to collect our casualty, a man with a spinal injury, who had been loaded on to the works stretcher. Gently placing it on top of ours we departed for the Royal Victoria Hospital with me steadying the stretcher, and the injured man's mates trying to comfort him.

Outings
We used to have staff outings but we couldn't all go together, of course, so we had two trips, a week apart. The blokes did overtime to cover each other's shifts. One of the places we went to was Perry Wood near Selling – a lovely spot in the country where the Salvation Army used to hold services. There was an open-air pulpit and there are pictures of fellas sitting by it with their pints of beer! Rosa and I used to go there for picnics. On one of these staff outings we were going off in an Orange Coach but our coach got stuck in the mud on Epsom racecourse. Another coach and driver was sent from London but he didn't know his way around. Fortunately, Joe had got his map. I remember the coach coming across the bit by Smallhythe and I said, 'Steady up, mate, there's an 'L' turn here and you'll be straight in the dyke if you don't make the corner!' We met a herd of cows and somebody said, 'What made you come this way, Joe?' So I said, 'They weren't on the map!'

Perry Wood pulpit, tramway outing 1922

The end of the line

On 31st December 1936 the last tram with passengers ran. It was cheered all the way to the Maxton depôt with Mayor Norman and official driver Percy Sutton at the controls. Also present was Fred Pay who drove the first Maxton tram 39 years earlier. I went up on the last tram to Buckland. My mate was given the job of putting the five open-topped trams on the sleeper track at River. We put them out there one at a time, walking back to Buckland each time to collect another. We sang Auld Lang Syne round the last tram outside the depot before it went. I can claim to have travelled on the very last one to move under power, when number 23 was driven out on to the sleeper track and we walked back to Buckland to phone the Electricity Works to cut the juice off for the last time. Then up the next morning to take the first bus out to make the 5.28 a.m. from Buckland.

Chapter 5

ON THE BUSES

I was one of the first to get a driving licence in 1936 when driving tests were introduced. My mother was pretty shrewd. She asked whether I would like to learn to drive for my 21st birthday because I might need to drive when the trams packed up. How she found the money I shall never know. I had a few lessons with a man who had a garage at the bottom of Coombe Valley Road where Graham's is now. I remember him saying, 'If you leave your foot on the clutch, I'll stamp on it!' He was a very good teacher. I failed the first time because I acted on somebody else's signal and I did my three point turn the wrong way. The blokes at work were all interested to know what you had to do to pass the test – not many people knew! I passed the second time. We bought this old 1926 Clyno car for £10. It was

Joe's 1926 Clyno

coach-built with a bench seat in the front and I remember once going round the lanes on the Romney Marsh and sliding right across the seat! I managed to clock-up 6,000 miles in nine months. In those days you had to have side and tail lamps on at night if you were parked on the road and so you had a flat battery every morning but I managed to get garage space at 2/6d. a week. All this driving stood me in good stead later because I was able to get my PSV (Public Service Vehicle) licence at the first attempt.

As tram employees we worked for Dover Corporation but East Kent took us over when the trams stopped and gave us all jobs on the buses. When I started bus conducting I went on the River route with single deck buses. It rained for a fortnight and it was standing room only with everybody wanting to go by bus. It was hell. I started at five in the morning, off from 10.30 to 11.30 on again until half past three. Fitting in a mid-day meal was a problem but my mother cooked my meal for 10.30. At half past three all I wanted to do was go to sleep – dog tired!

Tilling Stevens B49 C2 single-decker, new in 1931

Bus driver

East Kent decided that some of the younger ones could be trained up as driver/conductors for the smaller twenty-seaters. I always remember it. We did odd training runs with Brian Taylor who gave us instructions through the window. He put us in for our test because we were doing quite well, but the test came through in one week instead of the usual three. He said to me, 'You've got your test Monday morning, Joe,' 'But I haven't reversed yet,' said I. So Brian told me to come in Sunday morning and shunt some buses around ready for the next morning. One of the drivers came up to me and said 'You're working for no money against union principles!' I told him where to get off! I wanted to pass my test. I never crashed any and passed my test first time the next morning.

We had snow in early 1937 and there were problems at the bus stop outside St. Mary's Church. Spare staff from the garage were sent to clear the snow as the buses were having difficulty stopping and moving off. This was a notorious place for skidding on the wood blocks and I remember one bus demolishing the cast iron lamp standard outside the church. The covered arcade outside the Plaza cinema suffered the same fate.

There was another trouble spot when it was icy at the Crabble junction going out of

Clearing snow outside St. Mary's Church, 1937

town. Orders were given that buses were not to stop until they reached the top of the hill. One disgruntled passenger complained but the conductor explained that the boss, Mr Taylor, had given the instruction; the passenger retorted that he would like to sort out Mr 'B' Taylor! When the bus reached the top of the hill, another passenger alighted and introduced himself as Mr 'B' Taylor and asked the man, 'What would you like to do to me?' The bus went on its way with a very amused conductor!

After a spell as a driver I decided to become a bus mechanic. I never did an apprenticeship but I mended a lot of buses and kept them going through the War.

The War years

I registered for the Royal Air Force on the outbreak of the Second World War but every time I got my calling up papers they were cancelled because I was an essential worker being a mechanic who could do any job on the buses. Nevertheless, I spent the war years from 1939 to 1945 in uniform and under fire for quite a part of that time, but the uniform was that of the bus company. At the end of August 1939 there was a mad rush to conform to the blackout regulations by masking headlights and dipping the interior bulbs in blue paint. Reservists and 'Terriers' were being recalled to the colours. There was a period when we started the day by taking workmen out into the countryside to erect larch poles in the fields to deter glider landings. A fellow driver and I spent two nights at a local drill hall with the intention of taking territorials out to repel paratroopers. The buses we were using were Kentish built Tilling Stevens petrol-engined vehicles which had no self-starters, and when cold it needed some effort on our part to swing them into action. If the ignition was not set accurately there was also the kick to anticipate.

When 1st January 1940 dawned we knew that some of us younger staff would be called up. I had my twenty-fifth birthday three days before this, and kept being deferred, due, I believe, to the need for buses for evacuation and troop movements. I was part of the maintenance staff but was often called upon to drive or conduct (or both) when staff were short or something extra was required.

The railway line was blocked between Dover and Folkestone and buses were used to provide a shuttle service to connect with trains. One day I was hurtling down the road from the *Valiant Sailor*, when some police appeared near the *Plough Inn* at the Dover Borough Boundary. I had been doing about 60 m.p.h. in neutral and so I slipped back into gear and reduced speed but I need not have worried about exceeding the limit. Later I was to discover that the police were waiting for King George VI, who was arriving to see the troops passing through Dover.

Refugees

In 1940, after the invasion of Belgium, there was the sudden arrival of refugees from that country. On 22nd May I was sent down with others to collect them with a double-deck bus. This meant reversing some 400 yards down the Prince of Wales Pier with an anxious look up at the sky in case a Stuka appeared on the scene. However, they were very much involved forcing our troops back to Dunkirk. When we reached the pier-head we could see the small fishing boats disgorging their human cargo of men, women and children of all ages. We ferried them up to our Town Hall to sort them into categories for onward movement. The government was very concerned about fifth-columnists and when the refugees had been interviewed they were given a label. One of the men was speaking to a mate of mine and his tag showed that he was en route for Pentonville!

When they had been classified we took them up to Priory Station for entraining to various destinations up the line. I can recall one woman with a young child going into hysterics when a plane went over. Her friends said that she had been strafed by German aircraft on the way to the coast. The next day we were collecting them from the Marine Station. The railway workers did a magnificent job and soon they were involved with the evacuation of our school children plus the arrival of our troops from Dunkirk.

On 24th May 1940, just before clocking off one evening, we had a message to pick up some Royal Marines from the Western Docks. Four Tillings were pressed into service, and we were on our way to Chatham with a very lively crowd. It transpired that they had been over to Boulogne wrecking the harbour installations, as the enemy entered town, and had been evacuated by the destroyer *Venomous*. On returning to Dover at about 5 a.m. I relaxed a little and must have started to doze off. I almost finished up in a house in Maison Dieu Road, but luckily I was able to wrench the steering round to avoid a sticky end as later the cleaners found live rounds and thunderflashes littering the bus floor.

During the Dunkirk evacuation we were constantly called on by the Navy. One trip was to return some of the crew of the *Ajax* who had been manning rowing boats on the beaches. It was grand to stand on the deck of a vessel which had chalked up a victory in the early days of the war. We were taken down into the Petty Officers' Mess and given steaming mugs of cocoa plus buttered toast. During this period I had to do a trip up to the Western Heights one morning about 6 a.m. and could see about 40-odd ships anchored off the Admiralty Pier. What a picture it would have made if I had had my camera. But there was a grim reminder when I looked out to the East to see the smoke billowing up from the oil tanks at Dunkirk.

The weather remained good at this time, and I recall some of us sitting outside the East Kent garage sunning ourselves, when there was a roar from above. It was a Messerschmitt, and as it dived over the Burlington Hotel it released a clutch of bombs chained together. By the time they landed near the Naval Depot ship *Sandhurst* we had disappeared down the bus repair pits. A destroyer, *HMS Codrington,* was hit and was towed away and beached. It stayed there until after the War and was used by some of the local lads as a diving platform.

HMS Sandhurst alongside HMS Codrington after the bombing raid

The *Sandhurst* was also towed away. The Admiralty then decided to move the destroyers to a safer port before the German long range guns on the French coast started shelling Dover.

On 12th August an explosive device landed about 200 yards from my home and I dashed up to Prospect Place to see if there were any casualties. While I was checking this out a second one landed by our railway bridge in St. Radigund's Road and we could see a plume of smoke. This was nearer to home, and so I returned to learn that two of our neighbours had been killed on the way to report at Buckland Hospital after the first bang. It suddenly dawned on us that it must be cross-channel shelling as the missiles came out of the blue without any warning. They were supposed to whistle but I only remember pieces of shrapnel screaming by after an explosion. Later on in the war, I was walking down St. Radigund's Road by the garden wall of Grove House, Guy Mannering's home, and heard what I thought was a pistol shot; I looked round to see chimney pots spinning off the house opposite as shrapnel passed over my head. Then I realised it was another bout of shelling and luckily the shell had landed in soft ground in the garden and not too close to the wall. Guy Mannering kept rainfall records for most of his life and his rainfall box was destroyed by a shell. When it was known that shelling had started a double warning siren was sounded, and then the 'All Clear' one hour after the last shell had dropped in the town.

When we had our own long-range guns in action it was unwise to be in the St. Margarets-at-Cliffe area. One bus crew returning from East Langdon were fortunate, as on arrival at the garage, they found that a piece of enemy shrapnel had gone through the side of the vehicle. One night when we were cycling through Hawkinge as our artillery began to fire some ten miles away, the road was as light as day. You could even see the angle of fire.

The East Kent garage was in the firing line and we were convinced that the Burlington

Bomb damage in Liverpool Street, 11th September, 1940 with the Grand Hotel on the right. East Kent garage is behind the building on the left

Hotel tower was used by the gunners aligning their weapons. One night when staff were re-fuelling the buses, they saw the upper storeys of the tower disappearing in a cloud of smoke. We often sat in the repair pits listening to the shrapnel skating across the concrete floor.

We had rather a bad day on 11th September 1940 when a stick of bombs landed rather too close for comfort. One wing of the Grand Hotel was completely demolished. The *Sussex Arms* became a heap of rubble with a large crater in St James's Street about seventy yards from our blast- and splinter-proof shelter. After the dust had settled we emerged to investigate, including myself with the First Aid bag over my shoulder. Realising it was beyond our capabilities, I ran up to the First Aid Post skirting the bomb crater and told them of the extent of the damage. I was politely informed that they could not move until instructed by Central Control! We then extricated some residents from cellar shelters, and I recall one very large lady covered in soot proclaiming what she would do to Adolf if he ever arrived in Dover. The office girls cleaned her up and gave her a cup of tea while I applied sticking plaster to minor cuts. Hitler was supposed to have said that he would set up his HQ in Dover Castle, and I believe this was why it was not severely damaged. The Italian Air Force *did* score a hit on it but I believe that they were never sent across the Channel again.

Saved by the Home Guard

A Home Guard Transport Column was formed from members of the East Kent staff, and by 1942 we were getting into training. I still hadn't fired a rifle because we hadn't got them! During off-duty periods we had classes in map reading and small arms. Being able to map read from my Boy Scout days and able to drive probably saved my life because it meant that one weekend I was sent on an exercise instead of working. On Sunday 22nd March four of us caught a train to Maidstone and joined up with an R.A.S.C. Unit at Aylesford Priory. We were warned to be ready for an exercise that night, and I was detailed to go with a regular on a TCL (Bedford Troop Carrying Lorry). My mate was only too pleased to let me do the driving, and that night we camped on a village green. Next day we moved off and were 'ambushed', losing our first three lorries. We were No. 4 and I was presented with my mate's rifle, to hold off the enemy, while he reversed the vehicle. I crouched behind a hedge and aimed the weapon in the right direction, and could well have shot the umpire, but we managed to get away.

On returning to our huts, we were being fed when I picked up a newspaper lying on the table and read about a heavy raid on a South Coast Town with casualties at a garage. With some foreboding I managed to nip down into Aylesford village to a phone box. I rang our

Joe in Home Guard uniform, 1942

depot number, and was told to ring Buckland Paper Mill at 7 p.m. That sounded ominous. As I left the box I met our foreman and passed on the message. Later he came to the billet in a very distressed state to say that our boss and ten other members of the staff had been killed. The bomb had dropped at a quarter to ten and I should have been on the 2 till 10 shift. My uncle went down to the garage and tried to dig me out thinking I was on duty.

We caught a train back to Dover and reported at Buckland Tram Shed next morning. I had donned my overalls when I was told to conduct a bus until relieved. My tools had been salvaged by my workmates as my drawer had been smashed by shrapnel from the bomb. If I had been doing my normal shift I could have been standing there, and not able to record these events.

We were told that a bomb had dropped in the Market Square just after 9 p.m. destroying the Enquiry Office and killing the inspector on duty; fortunately all buses had already left on their last journeys. At about a quarter to ten another bomb was dropped on the garage close to the surface shelter, blowing out the walls and bringing down the concrete roof. Only the cufflinks of one chap were found. We reckoned that the bomb fell straight on him. All those in the shelter were killed except one, who was blown through a gap as the roof came down. During the following week we who had Home Guard uniforms carried our comrades to their last resting places. I carried to his grave my very good friend Bill Ford

East Kent Garage, 23rd March, 1942

who had been doing my shift whilst I was on exercise! That's how the Scouts and map reading saved my life. The only one to come out of that shelter alive was Nobby Clarke who became my best man later. He was injured with a broken femur but they saw his woolly hat that he always wore on the late shift and dug him out.

Based at Seabrook
The Russell Street garage was wrecked and arrangements were made to disperse the vehicles to Deal and Cheriton garages. The single-deckers went to Deal and the double-deckers to Cheriton where I went. I had to get there by bus. I started night-shift at Cheriton and then moved down to Seabrook. This garage had been built across the platforms of a branch railway line which never reached Folkestone. The depot had been immobilised due to the fear of invasion as it was right on the coast. The large fuel tanks had been filled with sand, and we were presented with an old tank waggon to replenish the buses. I

missed the first night there, but those on duty had been instructed to use five gallon cans and a funnel. It took all night with much fuel being spilt on the floor due to lack of light. Something drastic seemed indicated, and I discovered that the fuel hose from the tanker would fit into the filling orifices of the buses. I then dipped the tanker and recorded the number of gallons of diesel. The fuel would only flow when the air inlet on the tanker was open, and so a piece of cord was tied to the lever on top. The bus was brought into position, the hose inserted and the cord pulled. By listening we could gauge when we had put in sufficient fuel and the air vent was closed. After completing the fuelling operation, I dipped the tanker and found that about 140 gallons had been delivered, and so in the records I allocated about twelve to fourteen gallons to each vehicle. The powers-that-be did not interfere and I assumed that they could not think of a better way. This went well until someone did not check the cut-off mechanism and some went down the drain. I realised we had lost about ten gallons and so I added (on paper) a gallon here and there for about a week to cover this.

One night when bringing a bus over from Dover we were held up halfway to Folkestone. One of our planes had limped back across the Channel, crash-landed on the clifftop near Court Wood House and slid down across the main road. Eventually I had to drive the bus over a mound of earth, and when we reached Folkestone the place was deserted. We later learnt that a bout of shelling had just finished. One night I was taking a bus over to Seabrook and the engine failed at the bottom of Folkestone Hill. I realised that I was out of fuel but had a reserve of half a gallon but it still wouldn't go. I took out the cloth filter which was covered in gunge and then it started and I got to Seabrook on the half gallon.

On a Sunday morning I used to drive my staff back to Dover, and I remember passing Christ Church, Folkestone, at about 9 a.m. on 17th May. Shortly afterwards a hit-and-run bomber dived in and destroyed the body of the building. The tower still remains as a reminder of the narrow escape for us and the congregation.

I had nine months at Seabrook. I was there when the Dieppe raid was on and the whole building shook.

Back to Dover

With winter approaching it was decided to bring the buses back to Dover, as the hill up to the *Valiant Sailor* might become impassable during the icy weather. It was back to Buckland Tram Shed with some buses parked outside. Later we kept some of them in the derelict garage in Russell Street where we had re-fuelling facilities. On 25th October 1943 shelling made it very uncomfortable at Buckland. One shell had already landed at the back of the tram shed, by the Coleman Nurses' Home, setting an army vehicle on fire. I then gave the order to evacuate the buses and staff to River, about a mile further inland. The 'All Clear' did not sound until just after midnight, and we learnt that seven shells had landed in the Buckland area with nine dead and eight seriously injured. I still have the letter of commendation from the bus company for my prompt action.

This practice of parking the buses alongside River Churchyard became a regular feature, and then we had the problem of getting the vehicles running on cold winter mornings. It was necessary to drain the radiators and cylinder blocks overnight as we had some severe frosts. Our difficulty was to get hot water in the morning but we were not beaten. The old Tilling Stevens buses had large radiators needing about twelve gallons of water. We took one of these old faithfuls out, draped a sack over the radiator, and set up the throttle. We took two gallons of hot water out of the drain tap at the bottom and put two gallons of cold in the top. The system worked with water from the toilets, and an emergency fire tank in reserve. What a performance, but it worked. The things we had to do. There is still a little road island at that River terminus turning point and on one occasion I was carrying two cans of water, tripped and fell flat on my face. I was lucky I didn't scald myself. Most of the people in River had left so nobody complained about the noise at night. We started one bus up and its big end went – that was the end of that one for a while. On another night some idiot forgot about the low bridge at Kearsney and tried to take a double decker through – it didn't do the bus much good.

When shelling was going on the buses would stop at Maxton or Buckland. The point was, if you kept the buses running while the shelling was going on, people waited at the bus stops. At Cherry Tree a shell dropped on the bus stop with people waiting in the queue. We did the same with the miners' buses coming back to Dover from the pits. We wouldn't go into the town until the shelling stopped. We had a new inspector drafted in to us and he said that he would drive the miners' bus down. His name was mud because it was idiotic. He was down at Pencester and the buses were out at River, so he cycled up the town by Chitty's Mill at the same time as Jerry dropped a direct hit on the chimney of Chitty's Mill and the whole lot came down and blew him off his bike. By the time he got out to River he was a nervous wreck and we never saw much of him after that! That taught him not to ignore the shelling.

One night a driver rang me up and said, 'The shelling's finished. I'm off duty and I'm going home. I've left the bus at Maxton.' So I went off in a lorry to get it back. Well, we had had shells and bombs that night and every blooming road I went up had a bomb crater. I had to turn a double-decker bus round each time – not a three-point turn but about a twenty-point turn! It took me about an hour and a half to get from Maxton to Buckland.

Mobile staff canteen, 1943 (a Whorwell photograph)

We used to run a bus for the gun crews at Fan Bay and one night we had shelling and a driver rang me up and said, 'I'm off duty now. I've left a bus up a bank at Fan Bay.' A soldier with a torch was showing me the way when shelling started and he dropped the torch and ran off saying, 'It's up the bank, if you want it you can go and get it!' It wasn't a healthy spot!

We had a call that one of the old buses, a Tilling, had broken down at Guston. It was the halfshaft. You knew what tools you needed and we had a spare halfshaft in the stores. I put everything I needed on a single deck bus and drove out to Guston and unloaded it. I took off a bit of barbed wire that was clinging to the single-decker, sent it on its way and got on with the halfshaft job. After about 20 minutes a bloke came along on a bike and said my single-decker was stuck outside the Duke of York's School with something underneath the gearbox. Somehow I had hooked a barbed wire road barrier on to the bus and dragged it for a quarter of a mile!

Coming off duty after a night-shift I felt pretty rough and made an attempt to see Dr. Dick at the Royal Victoria Hospital. I was feeling so ill that I crawled home and went to bed at about 11 a.m. The next thing I remembered was that it was 11 p.m. and I should have been on duty at 10 o'clock! I had a high temperature and knew I had to report sick. Going out in the black-out, I put my hand out to open the gate, but it wasn't there and I was sure I was delirious. Next day I was told that during the day my iron fence had been smashed down with sledge-hammers while I was having a good long sleep and both the fence and gate had been removed as part of the war effort! After the War I replaced the fence using old cave air raid shelter bunks that were available for a reasonable price.

The Home Guard Transport Column had an exercise when we travelled from Margate to Sheldwich using mainly Tilling vehicles. A number of the engineering staff, including myself, followed up in a lorry to deal with breakdowns. Just behind was a mobile Bofors AA (ie anti-aircraft) gun trying to keep up with the convoy but this was left far behind when we were attacked by Whirlwinds dropping flour bags.

I had started to ride the Home Guard motorcycle about this time, and it was suggested that I get some night riding practice. On the evening of 4th June 1944 I changed into battle dress, rode out to Lydden and decided to go up Swanton Lane. I knew there was a landing strip at the top used by Air-Sea Rescue, but suddenly there was a roar and a plane dived and then others, and I nearly fell off my bike thinking the airfield was being attacked. Discretion being indicated I swung round and headed for home. Next morning D-Day was announced, and I realised that the activity was an attempt to deceive German radar by giving the impression of many planes taking off.

Relaxing in the mobile canteen, 1943 (a Whorwell photograph)

On our bikes

Rosa and I had a cycling holiday in the Cotswolds during the War. We came back by train but heard that Dover was being shelled heavily, so we decided to get off the train at Folkestone and cycle to Dover. However, at Ashford we were told that the shelling had stopped and people were leaving the caves. In fact the main shelling had stopped but one more came over. Fortunately, nobody was hurt. You didn't know when the shells were coming – they just arrived. So without any warnings, people carried on with their normal lives and if a shell had your name on it, that was that!

Bench Street, October 1943

Hitler's secret weapon

The 'flying bombs' or V1's were another hazard. My early memory of these was the remark of one of our drivers who used to get things a little confused, 'I saw one of them there planes with no "pirate" in it,' he said. One swung round over Buckland and returned to the sea, much to our relief.

Where are they now?

As the Allied armies occupied Germany there was the need for transport to convey the large number of displaced persons, for which a number of our Tillings were taken. I remember having to stay on to get our contribution checked over before their trip across the Channel. I often wonder where our old friends are now. I very much doubt if they ever returned, and are probably serving as henhouses or the like, somewhere in Europe.

The end of the War and the start of married life

I got married at St. Andrew's, Buckland in 1945. We were very friendly with the curate there. He was one of those who helped us out at the Guide cottage. A bus was out on test at the time of the wedding, pre-arranged, of course, and they cheered us as we came out of church.

I was still on the East Kent when the War ended and I decided to take exams. I took RSA exams, on bus operation. I've got a diploma upstairs. We had a new general manager who decided to start a local section of the Institute of Transport. I wrote and told him about my qualifications and he said that he would get me into the Chartered Institute, which he did. I keep thinking I'll pack it up; it's now called the Chartered Institute of Transport and Logistics! I was on the committee and spent a weekend at Ashridge College in Buckinghamshire.

Later I applied for a job as foreman of the Deal garage, but I knew I wasn't going to get it. The bloke who got it had no qualifications but because he was older than me he got first chance! In 1955 I went after a job at the Education Office as a schoolboard man for children playing truant. I didn't get it – apparently they didn't think I would stop because I had my Institute qualifications. Sometimes it doesn't pay to have qualifications.

At the same time, I put in for an ambulance job because I was so fed up with East Kent. They offered me twelve bob a week extra to stay. I was still on the mechanical side but I was being used as a relief on any shift because I could do anything. Also, a chest X-ray had revealed a shadow on one of my lungs probably caused by bus diesel fumes (fortunately it disappeared after I left the buses). So I gave in my notice. Then I had to move a bus. I saw this car draw out and so I backed thinking it was clear but I crashed into the boss's car. He thought I had done it on purpose, because I was leaving. I didn't do a lot of damage – just squashed the petrol tank!

Joe and Rosa's Wedding, 1945

Chapter 6

AMBULANCE MAN

After leaving East Kent the General Manager wrote to me offering me the chance of a job in Jamaica with Tillings, but I turned it down for family reasons and stuck to the ambulance job.

I got my First Aid qualifications from the Scouts when I was 17 and then kept it up with the St. John Ambulance. I was a member of the St. John Ambulance for five or six years after the War but my certificate had just run out when I got this ambulance job so I was six bob short until I went to a class and got my new First Aid certificate. I did a week's initial training without a uniform and went out on a major accident on the Alkham Road. This motor cyclist had gone under a bus and broken both legs. I was still in my civvy clothes! I was put in the back of the ambulance with the bloke. He lost one leg but survived.

On another occasion when I was still in my civvy clothes we picked somebody up on Crabble Hill and the policeman said, 'Is this your mother?' We had some fun one way and the other. It wasn't funny a lot of the time, of course, especially when it was kids. Some of the things you couldn't publish – like the poor soul who sat on the jerry, it cracked and she cut her bottom! We had to stick a plaster on her bottom! She worked in a shop in the High Street and I dared not go in there for weeks afterwards!

Baby on the way
There was a call one night that a woman was having a baby at the back of the Buckland tram sheds. I did wonder whether it was a hoax but when we got there she was standing on the pavement with her legs apart and the baby hanging down, howling its head off. We got her on to the stretcher and into the ambulance, then my mate, Bert, had to disentangle the baby from the mother's knickers! Her husband was taking her as a pillion pass-enger to his mother's where they were going to call the midwife. About a year later I was detailed to transfer a lady from Buckland Hospital maternity unit to the Royal Victoria Hospital. It was, 'Hullo, Joe. It's me again.' This time she had been involved in a car accident and had fractured a femur. Both babies survived their ordeals!

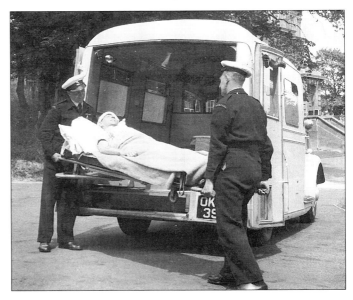

Bill Knott and Ronnie Russell loading an early Bedford ambulance with Mr Southey, a reporter

We did have some amusing experiences but others were deadly serious and when kids were involved it really hit you. We had to rush a child to hospital from Glenfield Road who wanted to take her favourite pillow, but she only survived a couple of days. I remember we were called to a child having a fit in Victoria Dwellings and I told a tenant that we needed to get the ambulance over to the doorway but the washing lines were in the way. In a trice she came out with a carving knife and the lines were removed. There were other sad cases that we could have helped more if only we had had the training and equipment available these days.

Somebody went over Shakespeare Cliff once and our new boss wanted an ambulance to drive from the Lord Warden Hotel across Shakespeare Beach to recover the person! Needless to say he had to give up and went on foot down the Sunny Corner steps!

Ships that pass in the night
One job which has to be dealt with at Dover is that of meeting patients being landed from passing ships. I well remember one stormy night when a patient was being landed at the end of the Eastern Arm. The steps were wet and greasy and with the motor-boat going up and down it was rather hair-raising. With one hand firmly gripping the hand rail we gave a final heave to land the wire stretcher, the delirious patient sat up, and we nearly all finished up 'in the drink'. After that the patients were brought into the more sheltered waters of the Camber.

Nowadays the stretchers have wheels and are of a reasonable height. At one time the main stretcher had to be loaded on to the near side of the vehicle and this could cause problems. Once we had a young lady who had fallen and dislocated her right elbow, and her arm was pointing out to the right and there was no way to give it support until we had her on the stretcher. We then realised that we could not load the stretcher in the normal way. We quickly switched the pillow to the other end and loaded her feet first. We had a rather similar problem when we were called to a footballer with a fractured lower leg. His team mate had attempted to splint the injury by using the corner flag as a support. As we loaded him I realised that we could not shut the doors with the red flag sticking out at the back. However his mates had not made too good a job of the bandaging and the flag fell out and so they were able to continue the game when I handed it back.

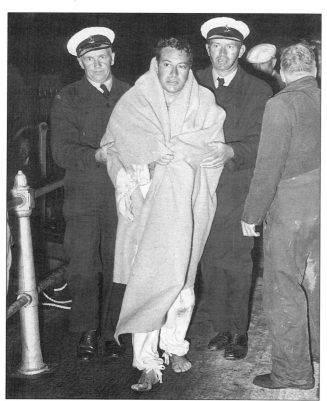

Joe, on the left, helps a Channel swimmer come ashore

Hungarian refugees

At the end of 1956 we were confronted with refugees fleeing from Hungary after the Russians moved in. Local people from many organisations rallied to assist and they included Red Cross, St. John Ambulance and the Women's Voluntary Service. On 19th November the Ostend boat arrived with 236 refugees which included 50 women and children. There were another 49 the next day and these were met by relief workers who attended to their needs and they were then sent onwards by rail. On 27th November 605 were helped on their way. The *Dover Express* on 30th November said that army barracks would be used to house up to 3,000. The troops were abroad involved in the Suez problem. On 7th December there were 1,300 refugees housed at the Connaught and Northfall Barracks, 200 more at Old Park Barracks and another 700 expected shortly. The local newspaper said that nothing like this had been faced by the town since Dunkirk. A very good friend of mine, Terry Sutton, a member of the Round Table, was given leave of absence by the local newspaper to organise entertainment for our visitors.

The Hungarians celebrate their Christmas on 6th December, St Nicholas' Day, and I was up at Connaught Barracks when they celebrated it on the eve with singing and dancing. Local organisations had raised money by various means and school children had found toys for the kids. The Army had provided food assisted by extra personnel from Guildford. The Red Cross ran the camps. The volunteer Red Cross nurses had problems with the language but luckily someone remembered that a matron at the Duke of York's School was fluent in the tongue, and some of the problems were solved. It was difficult to know what to supply for bottle-fed babies. Patients would not have the bedpan between the sheets and insisted on using it on the floor.

Morris ambulance about 1952

Then came the news that the troops were returning from the Suez conflict. My wife Rosa and I arrived at Old Park Barracks on Sunday 9th December with toys donated by fellow ambulance men to find everything on the move. Could we fold the blankets ready for the returning troops? On the Monday I was on Rest Day and went up to do some more bed making. Someone from the Red Cross came along to say they had a crisis. Could I take a party to Leighton Buzzard; so I was taken away from blanket folding. The St. John lady who was helping me said she would tell my wife I would be home much later. I went to the briefing and was allocated sixteen men for a hostel at Leighton Buzzard. Transport had been laid on, a coach took us to Dover Priory and I was issued with the rail tickets. On arrival at Charing Cross we were met by a small coach and were whisked over to Euston. Then there was the need for a toilet and I raced down the platform with half my gang. The train pulled in and I discovered it was non-corridor stock and that meant eight in each compartment. I changed compartments at every station but then there was another request for toilets. I cornered the guard, the train was held up, but I did not lose any of my party. On leaving the train we found another coach to take us to the Labour Hostel. Soon, I was on my way home with mission completed.

Three fifths of the staff around 1950: Ernie Hughes, Jack Hewitt and Wally Pascal

Promotion

The 'powers that be' decided to create the post of 'Senior Driver' to give an opportunity for promotion. Everybody was given the chance to sit an exam – more of an aptitude test than ambulance work. My map reading came in handy as they asked where certain places were in Kent. One of them was Chattenden. Have you heard of it? The only part of Kent that I didn't know was the Isle of Grain and I nearly put that as I had never heard of Chattenden, but I didn't! I was right. We had to do dictation which was all right as I was always good at spelling. I romped home and waited for the results. Eventually the word came round who had been offered the job and it was me. The Station Officer wanted somebody else; one or two were jealous and did all they could to make me chuck it in. Later on the Chief Ambulance Officer came to visit and told me that I was top in the county, but I never told the blokes at work! They kept changing the title of the senior driver after that. I never got much overtime as a senior driver because I couldn't fit the shifts in with my office job, so I was worse off than before. Overtime was your holiday money. In the end they promoted me to Assistant Station Officer and I was a bit better off then as well as having an officer's uniform with pips. When I opened up my uniform when I first got it, it was marked 'portly'. I had to laugh!

One lunchtime I was in charge with one ambulance on station. RAF Manston rang to say that their helicopter was following a yacht in distress and might have to lift the man off. Then the fun started! Connaught Barracks parade ground was the normal landing spot but the police had filled it with TIR lorries because of a hold-up in the docks due to the storm. Nobody had bothered to inform Manston! I knew that we had used the Granville Gardens but the police were not keen; so I tried the Duke of York's School, but it was lunchtime and there was nobody answering! I contacted the Council for permission to use Crabble Athletic Ground, but they refused because somebody might be walking their dog! Poulton Valley was then tried, but it was full of imported cars! Then RAF Manston rang again. The yacht had reached harbour safely!

Eventually I was the Controller. The Dover job was never advertised when it became vacant because they knew who they were going to put in. This bloke, Bob, came down from Sevenoaks, with the new arrangements he was 'Administration' and I was 'Control' splitting the old job. One day a letter came and Bob told me that I had to take down one of my two pips, but I said, 'No Bob, I think it's you who has to lose a pip'; he came down from three pips to two, the same as me! It was almost too funny for words – we were equal rank.

Ambulancemen Stan Boyd, Ron Russell, Reg Reader and Joe Harman, about 1960

Retirement

There was a chance of retiring early at 64 under the job release scheme and they were also centralising ambulance control. If I had stayed, I would have been pushed around the county covering people on training courses. It was no good training me with only one year to go, so I applied to retire in the December. In the November I had this dreadful cough and thought I had better take a week off because every time I answered the phone to take an emergency call, I started coughing. So I had a week off – it was whooping cough – and I never went back. They always said if you lived by the gasworks you wouldn't catch whooping cough, but they'd pulled it down by then, hadn't they?

Twizzie's bedroom

Whilst working with the ambulance service I met Elizabeth Twistington-Higgins who had unfortunately contracted polio in the 1950s. She was taught to paint by holding the brush in her teeth. I wanted to show her some slides of a holiday in Switzerland but she could not see them; so, I had the bright idea of showing them on the ceiling of her bedroom at the Dover Isolation Hospital. One night I went up there and up-ended the projector and it worked, but one of the night staff came on duty and reported that a man was lying on the floor of 'Twizzie's' bedroom! Later, Elizabeth gave Rosa and me one of her paintings, a ballet scene.

A pair of legs

Towards the end of my days in the Ambulance Service there was an amusing incident when an attendant in an ambulance returning to the depot spotted a pair of legs sticking out of a gateway in Elms Vale Road. Naturally assuming that the person had collapsed, he told his mate to pull in and bring emergency equipment. He nipped back up the road and saw it was a man face downwards. On touching him he heard a voice saying, 'I am only trying to turn off my stopcock!' This story managed to get on radio's News Quiz programme.

The beginning of the ambulance service

I spent the last twenty-three years of my working life as an ambulanceman. After I retired I looked up old records to see what arrangements were made to get people to hospital in the closing years of the last century. In those early days transport of the injured and sick was not of the best, with the roads very rough, and the need to use any means that came to hand. The police were involved in most cases, and fortunately they had training in First Aid via the St. John Ambulance Association. I found in the Watch Committee Minutes a mention of 24 certificates being presented in 1894. A new stretcher was ordered in 1881 and in 1896 a new litter was purchased for the Hose Reel Station at Buckland for the price of £20.14s.6d. The Hose Reel Stations contained fire-fighting equipment and the litter (ie stretcher resting on wheels). The one in Union Road (now Coombe Valley) was a corrugated iron building and was situated just through the railway arch on the left on the way to the Union (now Buckland Hospital).

As the borough extended, further stations were built including one in 1908 at the top of 'The Cut' near the bottom of Whitfield Hill. A little later one was erected next to the Maxton Tramshed. During the construction of the harbour Messrs. Pearsons stated in 1898 that they had ambulances of the latest pattern at their two blockyards (no doubt the 1894 Furley Litter). The Furley Litters were also used to convey sudden deaths to the mortuary near the Clock Tower. This was the practice up to the outbreak of the last war and I can remember meeting them once near home, and was told later that it was an old photographic friend of mine who had passed away suddenly. In 1874 the Watch Committee made an

Furley litters with a horse-drawn ambulance behind (courtesy of John Gilham)

order for the inside of the skylight of the Dead House to be painted. I suppose this was to deter the local lads from getting a view of post mortems by climbing on the roof.

Furley Litters

Back in 1906 Canon Bartram had presented the St. John Ambulance Brigade with a Furley Litter in recognition of their kindness to his wife. Mr Hobday of Buckland Paper Mill purchased one for his employees due to the lack of local provision. I was told by his son that Cocky Miller enjoyed pushing his mates around! It was not until 1924 that the St. John Ambulance Brigade was presented with an ex-RAF Crossley ambulance, paid for by public

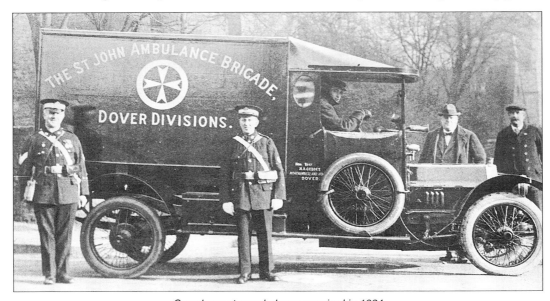

Crossley motor ambulance acquired in 1924

47

Chevrolet ambulance acquired in 1936

subscription. They later had an Austin followed by a Vulcan and Ford. By 1936 they had a Chevrolet, which was kept in a yard at the bottom of Union Road (now Graham's).

The Fever Waggon
The town had a horse-drawn Fever Waggon (similar to a Black Maria) after the First World War, and in 1921 a friend was placed in the top bunk. She succeeded in rolling off on the journey to the Isolation Hospital at Tower Hamlets. The horse was provided by Mr Nash when required. About a year later Mr Kirkwood, the driver, changed over to a motor vehicle, but early in 1922 I travelled in one of Mr Nash's carriages to the Noah's Ark Isolation Hospital. I had a letter from a lady who remembers contracting polio in 1911 at the age of three and being wrapped in a blanket and taken by her father to the hospital on a tram. During the polio epidemic soon after I joined the service in 1955 we were called to the Prince of Wales Pier to meet a tender. The patient had come from the Varne Lightship and we rushed him up to Tower Hamlets to put him in an 'iron lung'. This reminds me of the present fear of 'Aids' as the crew kept well away and let us do the unloading. We must have built up an immunity as none of the staff or families caught the disease.

River tram accident
In 1917 Dover was shocked by the tramway accident which took place one Sunday afternoon in August. As I was only two at that time I decided to consult the files of the *Dover Express* to find out how the large number of casualties were dealt with as there were 11 dead and 60 injured. From the reports it was obvious that the cause was an inexperienced driver, recently discharged from the Forces, failing to carry out the

recognised safety procedures. He should have stopped on the brow of the hill at Crabble (near the present traffic lights) and applied the slipper-brake which pressed on the running rail. He did not shut off power and so could not use the emergency brake, consequently tram No. 20 overturned at the bottom bend and, by striking a wall, it more or less wiped off the top deck passengers and seats. The first report came to the Tram Depot at Buckland when a lady ran in with a message from a railway signalman. The accident happened just below the bridge on the Canterbury-Dover line and it seems probable that the driver of a passing train stopped at the Bunkers Hill signal box and reported the catastrophe. The signalman in turn passed the message to a lady in an adjoining house who ran down the hill.

Inspector Elgar boarded the next car to River, and on reaching the top of the slope into River, he learnt of the severity of the accident. He disembarked the passengers and then took the tram down Crabble Hill with the most severely injured, although hampered by the lack of stretchers. They were then conveyed to the Royal Victoria Hospital in the High Street with two of the victims dying on the way. The *Cricketers Inn* was turned into a first aid dressing station, with local residents tearing up sheets to make bandages. Chief Constable David Fox received a 'phone call and put into operation a pre-arranged emergency procedure by alerting doctors and requesting help from the Army. He also sent the three-wheeled police ambulance. PC Booth was on the scene shortly after the event, taking control until his Chief arrived with two Union nurses. More tram cars were used to transport the injured as well as military ambulances with an army surgeon. Sergeant Gore and other members of St. John gave valuable help. There were a number of soldiers injured, and they were taken to the military hospital under the Western Heights. Trooper Gunner tried to stop the tram after the driver jumped off, but lost both feet in consequence, and in recognition of his bravery was awarded the Albert Medal. I should imagine the policemen were rather exhausted by the time they had pushed the litter from the Town Hall to Crabble at the double. The Market Hall was used as a mortuary in the same way as it was after the war-time Zeebrugge Raid.

River tram accident, 1917

Fourpence up and tuppence down

I have been told of an accident between the wars which took place on Castle Hill when a bus overturned on the hairpin bend. The police were assisted by a garage owner who provided an open vehicle which enabled them to place the stretchers crossways across the back seats with the constables holding them in place. This could have been the vehicle which provided a service to the Castle for fourpence up and twopence down. An old friend of mine remembers breaking his leg playing football at River at about the same time, and they endeavoured to get the St. John ambulance but it was out of town. He was then lashed to a wattle and placed across the back seat of an open tourer for his journey to hospital. There was also a car crash at Temple Ewell, with the injured being taken to hospital in the local butcher's horse-drawn cart. I believe it was in 1937 that Superintendent Marshall Bolt managed to arrange for the Chevrolet Ambulance to be stationed in a bay at the Fire Station and manned by the Police.

The end of the local ambulance service

During the war accidents were dealt with by the Civil Defence but that's another story. In the transitional period after the war an ambulance was kept outside a private house to answer night calls. The St. John Ambulance Brigade picked up the threads after hostilities had ceased, and ran a service for removals alongside a local government unit which dealt with accidents. The Kent County Council came into the picture after the National Health Act and the two amalgamated and were stationed at the Isolation Hospital. By the time I joined in 1955 the ambulance station had moved to the old Westmount College Stable Block off Folkestone Road.

Chapter 7

HOSPITALS

Dover has a very good Hospital League of Friends of which I can claim to be a founder member after attending an inaugural public meeting in 1955, chaired by Mr Proudler, the dentist. He pointed at me and several others and said, 'You are on the Committee!' and I'm still on it! As I remember, our first effort was to provide curtains round the beds, which meant that the nurses no longer had to drag round screens and the curtains gave a lot more privacy for the patients. The Hospital Broadcasting System was also one of our projects and I recollect going up to the old studio in the Isolation Hospital. The main fundraising event was, and is, the annual Hospital Fête held in Pencester Gardens which I organised for five years. Following closure of the Royal Victoria we now direct all our efforts towards the assistance of our only remaining hospital, Buckland. Even that is under threat.

George Dickinson's Brook House

Dover's old Royal Victoria Hospital in the High Street ceased to take in patients in 1987, and then gradually deteriorated until, fortunately, it was acquired by a housing trust which preserved the frontage whilst converting the interior to attractive living accommodation.

The original building was erected for George Dickinson, a paper-maker whose business was nearby, close to the River Dour. He also had connections with Bushy Rough and Buckland Paper Mills. About 1833 he set up a steam paper mill in Charlton and appeared to have had some very rash ideas, because five years later he was bankrupt. He had had this house built about 1834 and he was responsible for building Victoria Crescent opposite to preserve a good view. This residence was known as 'Brook House' – not to be confused with another of the same name built by Mr Moxon in 1860 and now demolished.

'Instituted at the General Thanksgiving of MDCCCXLIX' is the inscription on the front of the old house, and many passers-by today would be puzzled by the term 'General Thanksgiving'. But people in Dover in 1849 indeed had cause for thanksgiving because the town was fortunate enough to be spared the worst of the cholera epidemic which killed 53,000 people in England and Wales alone in that year. One result was that a fund was raised to provide a hospital. In 1850 Brook House came on the market and was purchased for £1,336. Many improvements were carried out over the years, but the first job was to replace the (presumably tarred) paper roof with slates. We should not be too surprised about the roofing material as the first tenant was a paper-maker.

People's Dispensary

The story of the hospital really starts in 1823 when an attempt was made to set up a People's Dispensary under the patronage of the Earl of Liverpool, the then Lord Warden. However, it was not until the Duke of Wellington took over as Lord Warden in 1829 that things began to move and premises were obtained off the Market Square at the back of what became Flashman's. Later they moved to Snargate Street and Queen Street. The Duke continued to be a patron for the rest of his life.

The dispensary was founded by local worthies for the benefit of the Sick Poor. An apothecary was appointed, who lived in, and was paid £80 per annum with 'coals and candles provided'. The Annual Reports from 1828 until 1947 are available in the Dover Reference Library and give much information regarding cases dealt with and rules applied. The 1835 Report defines the area within which its doctors would make home visits. It more or less covers the boundaries of the old town: 'From the boundary at the Pier by Archcliffe Fort on the North and West sides of the town by the Common. The footpath leading from Bowling Green Lane to the Priory Fields and along the Charlton Road by the house lately erected by George Dickinson Esq (later the hospital). It continues down Ladywell Lane into Maison Dieu Fields to the Gasworks.' This included the old parishes of St. Mary and St. James, up Charlton High Street, and later extended up to the Turnpike Gate (now Tower Hamlets traffic lights) and down Bridge Street into Charlton Green and turning right into Maison Dieu Fields.

In the first year 452 patients were treated, some in their own homes. Of these 311 were cured and 35 relieved, with 23 dying. The latter group included 11 with consumption, two from palsy and apoplexy, three with dropsy, plus one each 'water in chest' and 'water in head'.

The Dispensary was financed by subscription and collections in local churches. Those who contributed one guinea were Governors and for ten guineas you were a Life Governor. Finance was always a problem, for when you enlarge or take on more commitments running expenses rise. It is worth listing some of the ideas they had to provide more income: 'Received from a fine on John Fry for setting light to a field of gratten (stubble)' in 1827, 7/6d.; from Murray Lawes of Old Park 'donations from those skating on Frith Pond', and in 1870 there was a Whit Monday Fête at Kearsney. Collecting boxes were placed in public houses, and contributions came from various work-places. This developed into the Hospital Saturday Fund with a parade on the seafront. Special efforts were made to finance improvements but there was never enough cash and there was the threat of closing two wards. In more recent years there were Pound Day collections which started in 1903. As a Boy Scout between the wars I remember going round in one of Mr Husk's lorries collecting pounds of sugar and later eggs. It all helped the Dispensary to keep going.

Hospital opens
The hospital had opened on 30th May 1851 with Mr and Mrs Jarrett as Porter and Matron at £45 a year. A female servant was later allowed at £25 a year. In my research into the records of the Dover Police Force I found that Samuel Jarrett had resigned to take up a post at the hospital. There were nine beds and the costs that year were £125.2s.1d. Canon Puckle of St. Mary's had been involved since 1844 and was Chairman from 1863 until his illness in 1893. He was also Chaplain, but patients were allowed visits by their own cleric. Under Rule 16 patients were asked to give thanks in their own church when cured.

Expansion
Additions were made to the building in 1860 and in the seventies, with a new wing by 1890. In 1897 one of the women's wards was named 'Victoria' in honour of the Queen's Diamond Jubilee and used for children. It was at this time Dover College provided a cot and others followed suit. In 1898 the telephone was connected, and four bedrooms and a bathroom were provided for the nurses. Thanks to someone's generosity electric light was installed free of charge, and a Röntgen Rays (X-rays) apparatus supplied. In 1901 an operating room and lift were added in memory of Sir Richard Dickson, a former Mayor and a local wholesale grocer. When Edward VII succeeded Queen Victoria in 1901 he gave permission for the hospital to be called the Royal Victoria after his mother.

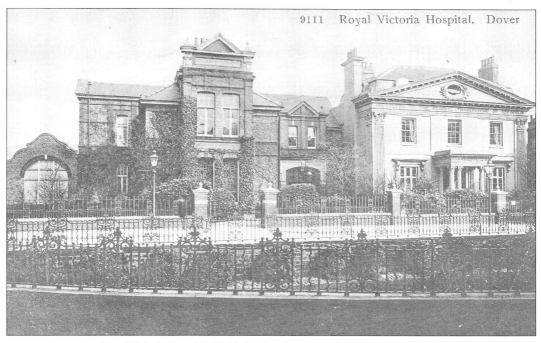

*Royal Victoria Hospital, 1917 showing the original house and the annexe
added in 1887 for Queen Victoria's Golden Jubilee*

Former Royal Victoria Hospital today

Isolation hospitals

The Noah's Ark Isolation Hospital was built on the hill at Tower Hamlets in 1871 and was in place for a smallpox outbreak in 1872. Later a smallpox hospital was built at Mount Ararat near St. Radigund's Abbey.

Troubled times

The beginning of coal mining in Kent in the early years of this century meant that more accidents had to be dealt with (the management contributed towards the hospital expenses), and the same applied when the National Harbour was under construction. There was a problem when the National Insurance Act was passed in 1911; income decreased and doctors were not prepared to treat insured persons free. The First World War disrupted the running of the hospital as air raids became more frequent. The Red House on the London Road, River, (now flats) was taken over as a relief hospital in 1917. An instruction was given that operations on less serious cases were to be postponed from the light or dangerous periods of the month to the moonless fortnight, so as to keep the hospital as free as possible for casualties during the former. The tramway accident in 1917 put a severe strain on the facilities as eleven casualties remained there for a considerable time. In 1919 a glass porch over the front entrance was provided with monies handed over after the war, and this survived until recently.

In 1927 a Centenary Fund was started for a new wing which came to fruition in 1933. Mr W.B. Brett organised the workers' collections and Mr Phillip Hart the Hospital Box collections. My mother was a box steward, my youngest sister worked for Mr Brett, and I was involved in repairing the boxes. Then there were the Hospital Fêtes, which started in the Dover College grounds in 1903 as a two-day event. Much later, I was the Fête organiser for five years.

Second World War

At the outbreak of the Second World War the patients were evacuated to the Waldershare Park Mansion, and the Coleman Nurses' Home became a military hospital. Buckland Hospital became a Casualty Hospital and was heavily involved during Dunkirk with the R.V.H. playing its part. The R.V.H. still dealt with casualties and was very busy with 'black-out' accidents in the early period until we developed better night vision – I well remember walking into a tree in Cherry Tree Avenue! There were plans in 1944 for a Battle of Britain Hospital with Princess Elizabeth as patron, but the 1946 National Health Act was the finish of that project.

The end of R.V.H.

Buckland Hospital had by now taken over medical cases, leaving the R.V.H. providing general and orthopaedic surgery beds together with an out-patient and casualty service. Gradually Buckland Hospital took over more and more as rebuilding took place, with orthopaedic wards going and surgical following when the former medical wards had been refurbished. This left the R.V.H. with a stroke unit and geriatric day hospital. In May 1987 it closed its doors.

A new workhouse at Buckland

Buckland Hospital was originally a workhouse. After the Poor Law Amendment Act of 1834 was passed, updating the original Elizabethan Poor Law legislation, the authorities decided to build a new workhouse on the outskirts of the village of Buckland. Access was by rough trackway up the Coombe Valley, later known as Union Road. They started levelling the ground for the building on 14th July 1835 and it took nine months to build, with the inmates moving in on 22nd April 1836. They had been transferred from the River and Martin institutions with the St. Mary's Poorhouse joining them in September of that year. This meant that further buildings were needed, which included an infirmary up on the terrace.

Dover Union in 1935 showing the original layout of the buildings before rebuilding work (courtesy of Dover Express)

The original workhouse, costing £6,374 4s 11 1/4d., was built on a plan approved by Sir Francis Head, the Poor Law Commissioner. It was in the form of a quadrangle with the Board Room and the Master's offices in the front over the entrance and a small hospital against the opposite wall, the rest of the square being occupied by the ward rooms and dormitories. It was very like a prison, with none of the windows affording an outside view. There were dividing walls across the square. The control of the Union Workhouse was under a Board of Guardians and the inmates were grouped under four classes: casuals or tramps, the able-bodied, the aged and the sick. Many of these unfortunate people had nowhere else to go due to lack of employment and consequent destitution. It was the policy in the early days to scare people by the harsh regimes in order to reduce the cost of out-relief paid from local rates.

A tramp, applying for admission, was asked his name, his age and birthplace, where he had come from and where he was going. He was given a bath and kept for one day during which he was employed in gardening, breaking stones or chopping wood. There was a long report about the Workhouse in the *Dover Express* of 25th April 1902, but no mention of the casuals.

Iron mothers

While checking through old copies of the *Dover Express* I found the mention of an 'Iron Mother' in the Board of Guardians' reports. This was a large pestle and mortar used for breaking stones by the itinerant visitors to the Union in lieu of payment for their board and lodging. When first introduced it was said to be useful in deterring tramps from heading this way. It must have had some success as there was an item in the next report to say that

Rebuilding work 1936, Buckland Hospital

they had bought six more at £3 a time. Quite a number who finished their days in the workhouse were buried in Buckland Cemetery.

There were further enlargements in 1849 and 1871. The extension of the hospital wing took place in 1897. The Editor of the *Dover Express,* writing in 1907, said that, 'as it stands the principal feature of the House now is its hospital, consisting of a long range of buildings on the upper terrace extending from boundary to boundary. The conditions of Poor Law Administration have now so changed that the House is now mostly needed for the sick, the aged and for children'.

In 1913 the Guardians decided that all the children over the age of three should be boarded out. The workhouse school had been closed for some time with the children attending Buckland School. The workhouse children stand out in the school photographs with their pinafores and shaven heads.

In 1929 a Local Government Act was passed and the care of the poor of Dover was transferred to the Kent County Council. In 1936 much work was carried out to the front of the building.

Casualty hospital
It became a casualty hospital during the 1939-45 war, and it did outstanding work during the Dunkirk period. Dr Gertrude Toland was one of the heroines of that time. The hospital was lucky not to be damaged during the war but it had some close shaves with a bomb which landed on the trench shelters which are still there underneath the car park, and there was a landmine on Randolph Road close by which caused a considerable number of deaths.

National Health Service
The National Health Service Act of 1946 started to change things and gradually services were transferred from the 'Old Vic' to Buckland. When I joined the Ambulance Service in 1955 moves were underway. This meant the stripping out of the old blocks on the terrace and creating the new Churchill and Ramsay Wards. At the same time they put in the lifts which were a great boon to us ambulance men after years of struggling up the winding stairs to the old medical wards. I believe the Casualty Department was one of the last units to move. Before the 1939-45 war there was a plan to build a road over the hill to Tower Hamlets and so make the hospital more accessible, and the ground was prepared by giving work to the unemployed. The ground is now covered with bushes and weeds on the left of the roundabout. We must remember that when the workhouse was first built it was at least half-a-mile from any habitation, and that the trackway was only for horse-drawn vehicles. We are now suffering from the lack of access and the addition of the industrial estate on the site of the old rubbish tip. I also recall the mileage I might have saved by routing ambulances over the hill to Buckland when I was Control Officer at the Ambulance Station.

With constant reorganisation Buckland Hospital always seems to be under threat. I think back to the people who worked so hard to raise money to provide the facilities, and my mother's work with others on the Hospital Box Committee in the 1930s. The hospital chapel was built by public subscription and is now the restaurant, but we now have St Luke's Chapel on Churchill Floor. Gradually various services have been transferred to the William Harvey Hospital at Ashford. The Casualty Department has become a Minor Injuries Unit. Emergency cases are taken to Ashford for treatment. This has brought further pressure on the Ambulance Service. Visiting patients at Ashford is another problem. As Dover is a major port it does not seem logical to reduce services.

Part of the original workhouse in 1960

Buckland Hospital 1960 from the lift shaft. Chapel in foreground

Chapter 8

ST. MARY'S CHURCH AND ITS RESTORATION

I didn't get involved with St. Mary's until the Second World War. Rosa helped to run the Guides at St. Mary's before the War and went back after the War. She roped me in to do things; I was one of the assistants, testing them on map reading and things like that.

I went to Sunday School for a while at Buckland, but then I had diphtheria and my mother said, 'They never came to see how you were when you were so ill, so you're not going back there!' Then I joined the Scouts at Charlton and I became server and candleboy. I was never in the choir – I'm no good at singing, but that didn't stop me going on the choir outings! I was on the Parochial Church Council, too. My uncle was churchwarden at Buckland and his wife said, 'Old Joe is living on his own, perhaps he'd like to sleep at our place'. So I moved in there for a while during the War and went to St. Andrews, breaking my links with Charlton. Meeting up with Rosa who went to St. Mary's meant that I started going to St. Mary's. I still remember all the windows boarded up and the candlelit services. Canon Cooper came in 1943. St. Mary's used to elect their new vicar but the elections got quite dirty. On one occasion a candidate was a vicar from Hastings and no way were they going to let a vicar from Hastings come to St. Mary's – there was always rivalry between Dover, the premier Cinque Port and Hastings which also claimed the honour. Anyway, Canon Puckle decided that these elections should finish; he consulted the Archbishop and put a stop to them in 1870. Puckle died in 1894. Canon Elnor, who was Vicar during the First World War, retired just before the Second World War and Canon Ritchie was appointed. It is said that Canon Ritchie guided his flock during the War. I never met Ritchie, but somebody told me that you never saw him for dust when things got hot! Canon Purcell took over until Cooper came who was quite a nice old boy.

It is Canon Puckle who was very much responsible for what St. Mary's looks like today. It must have been the talk of the town when, in July 1843, it became known that they were going to pull St. Mary's Church down. There

Harold Dolbear and Joe, Charlton Church Choir outing to Winchelsea in about 1928

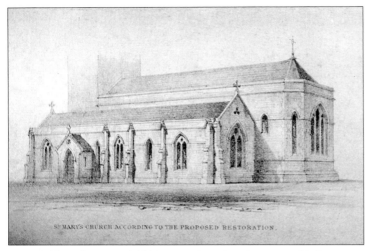
Plan of proposed 1843 restoration; clerestory was added

must have been a number of locals looking over the hoardings, especially when they started to remove some of the former Dovorians in order to reinforce the foundations, which had been dug away over the years for burials.

St. Mary's early history

The oldest parts of the church are the Norman arcades and the lower part of the tower, which may have been a narthex or porch to the building. As you enter the church you may notice that the arches on the right or south side are eighteen inches higher than those on the north, but appear to be the work of one stonemason. The original building was small and would seem to have ended with an apse connecting the two double pillars. It was extended eastward with more pillars of almost identical design of which two remain. Around this time three more stages were added to the tower. The arches on the north side of the chancel are Early English as is the window on the south side.

There is a possibility that the original building was a hospice for pilgrims which came under the jurisdiction of the Master of the Maison Dieu when that was built in 1203 by Hubert de Burgh. The priests were provided by the Master up to the Dissolution in 1537 when the church was closed. The town church had been St. Peter's in the Market Square which was used by the Mayor and Corporation for elections but this was in a neglected state. The townsfolk implored Henry VIII to let them have St. Mary's as a parish church and, after this was granted, the Mayor and Councillors transferred from St. Peter's.

Photography had not been invented long enough to give us pictures of the church in 1842, but we have water-colours and drawings to give us some idea of the state of the building. For many years the church had only been patched up and the windows were of poor quality according to drawings that have survived. In 1804 the church authorities decided to remove a pillar from each side and to throw an arch over the gap to give a better view of the pulpit. There was also a plan to remove another two pillars, but this was never carried out. The Mayor and jurats sat at the east end behind

Watercolour of St. Mary's Church, 1792

the altar and used it as a table during elections. In 1829 the noted antiquarian, Sir Stephen Glynne, visited the church and recorded his opinions but these were not published until after his death at the age of 66 in 1874. He said, 'The exterior has been sadly modernised and many frightful windows inserted,' adding that a clerestory would improve it as the roof was too low. The tower arch had been blocked off with solid whitewashed timber and the Norman arcades filled in with brickwork. This included the gallery for the pilots and choir and a 'non-speaking' French organ.

Watercolour of N.W. corner of St. Mary's, 1842

Victorian restoration

The Rev. John Puckle came to Dover in 1838 as a curate to the Rev. John Maule and was elected as Vicar to succeed him in 1842. In 1843 he decided with the assistance of his very good friend, Dr William Sankey, a retired Army surgeon who had settled in Dover in 1814, that something must be done to preserve the fast deteriorating church. The pillars supporting the arches constructed in 1804 were showing signs of stress due to the additional thrust. There was the possibility that it might be necessary to demolish the whole building and start from scratch, but Puckle and Sankey had other ideas. After stormy battles at vestry meetings where most were only in favour of patching up the building, a compromise was reached, and the authorities agreed to spend £1,600, but the ardent restorers had to raise the balance of at least £3,000. The final vote was 160 for restoration and 58 for 'desolation'. Mrs Sankey immediately gathered round her a band of willing helpers who raised over £350 at a bazaar held at the Apollonian in Snargate Street.

It would have been cheaper to build a completely new nave and chancel but the Canon was determined to retain the Norman and Early English work. Work started on 24th July 1843 and when the old box-pews had been removed it showed up the danger of the imminent collapse of the building. Over the centuries burials had taken place inside, which meant the floor was honeycombed with graves and, to squeeze in the last few, the pillars had been undermined. About four feet down the remains of a Roman bath-house with its hypocaust were exposed under the Norman pillars. These were taken down and the stones

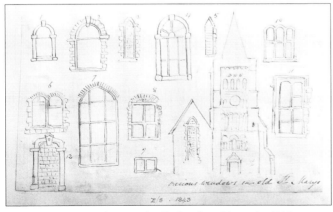

Windows referred to by Sir Stephen Glynne in 1829

61

Interior after removal of the box-pews and galleries

numbered for eventual replacement. Then the foundations were reinforced with about 15 feet of concrete. There was a big argument with the builder over putting back the Early English window, the Ship Window, in the south wall of the chancel. He offered various alternatives, but eventually it was put back, for which we must be thankful. I often take visitors up there to admire both the window itself and the image of the old *Invicta* ploughing across the Channel.

The tower arch was rebuilt but it still has a depressed look to this day. The restorers thought that this was its right shape, but later experts suggest that it was originally semi-circular, but had felt the weight of the extra stages added to the tower. More work was needed on the tower, but this had to wait until 1898 when two large cracks were found in the upper stages so that the bells could only be tolled, but not rung, for over fifty years. The remains of the old Purbeck marble font were discovered in the walls and were expertly joined together and put on a new base. The damage to it could have happened in the Commonwealth period, but there does seem to be a possibility that a part of it protruded from the wall at the west end. Pillars were put back to replace those removed in 1804 and the clerestory added, improving the interior proportions and the lighting.

When the present pews were put in there was a block up the centre for the poorer parishioners. These were removed in 1913 and used to extend the side benches, and this can be seen on close scrutiny. Galleries were provided on each side but were removed in recent years. The Mayor and Corporation were persuaded to move up into the northern gallery. During the rebuilding of St. Mary's, services were held in the Maison Dieu which had not yet been restored.

Many ancient churches restored in the Victorian era were completely rebuilt, so we must be thankful that the most interesting parts of St. Mary's were retained.

Christ Church

The 'Opposition', or Low Church fraternity, left and acquired land in Folkestone Road to build a new church. They wasted no time and the foundation stone was laid by the Vicar of Hougham, in whose parish it was, on 2nd August 1843 and it was consecrated on 13th June 1844. This was three months before the reconsecration of St. Mary's and so it was claimed that Christ Church was older than St. Mary's! Christ Church was demolished some years ago and a block of flats now occupies the site. When they were digging the foundations for the flats they discovered a coffin encased in lead in a brick vault. After persistent research it was discovered that it was that of the Rev. Thomas Morris, who had laid the foundation stone in 1843. He has now found his last resting place in the village churchyard at Hougham.

Doctor William Sankey and Canon Puckle

Doctor William Sankey FRCS came to Dover in 1814 after retiring from the Army due to ill-health and became a well-respected resident of the town and a councillor. He must have been very fond of St. Mary's and backed John Puckle when he became Vicar and had a vision to restore the church. It would not be here now if the pair had not pressed on with the project. William died in 1866 and was buried at East Langdon with his forbears. It is still possible to see his memorial there.

Rev. John Puckle was promoted to Canon, probably in the 1860s, and died in 1894 after

Joe at the 1993 exhibition at St. Mary's

63

over 50 years at St. Mary's. There is a wall painting of the Epiphany on the west wall which was commissioned to celebrate Canon Puckle's fifty years of ministry in 1888. In 1889 he was presented with a piece of silver and £1200 by grateful parishioners and townspeople. He was a great worker for the Dover Hospital and was Chairman of Governors from 1863 until just before his death. He has at times been blamed for the way in which he restored the church, but from all reports in the newspapers he was greatly loved, and many Dovorians attended, including the Mayor and Corporation, when he was laid to rest in St. Mary's Cemetery. His gravestone was damaged by a shell during the Second World War, but I was able to clean it up to read the inscription. In the vestry you will see an oil painting of the man whose enthusiasm saved an ancient church for future generations.

Oil painting in the Vestry of Canon Puckle, 1813-1894

The bells

There is more to tell about work on the tower in 1898 which included refurbishment of the ring of eight bells which had only been tolled for about sixty years. The tower had to be strengthened and the bell-frame supported on wooden pillars. The treble had to be recast and the other seven quarter-turned. We now face the need to eighth-turn the bells to keep them pealing. I am not an expert on bells but this treatment will mean that the clappers will strike a different spot avoiding the worn faces. All that is needed is £100,000!

Chapter 9

BUCKLAND VILLAGE

I have lived in St. Radigund's Road in the parish of Buckland all my life. It did not get that name until 1865 after the railway arrived. Prior to that it was known as Butcher's Lane. A local butcher, Mr Quested, owned land in the area and may have had a slaughter-house in the vicinity. Buckland village has now been overtaken by the spread of Dover, and has to some extent lost its identity in the process. When I was told that another historian considered that there was nothing of interest in Buckland, I started looking around, determined to prove him wrong.

I had studied the 'Burial Records of Buckland in and near Dover' from 1857 onwards which gave much information as to tradesmen. I followed this up with census returns, the evidence of my own eyes and scraps of information gleaned over the years.

Buckland in Dover
Many people have passed through Dover and have continued up the London Road towards Canterbury and beyond. At one time the old town of Dover consisted only of the parishes of St. Mary's and St. James's, with the dividing line being the River Dour. It seems that for many years the route inland for horsemen and walkers was to the east of the river, but with the coming of the coaches a turnpike trust to Barham was created in 1753, which made the road up to Buckland to the west of the river. Hasted records a newly-built bridge, Buckland Bridge, and the *Bull Inn* nearby dates from about that time. From about 1800 some of the

William Burgess print (about 1840-60) of Buckland Bridge built about 1800 (replacing a ford) and The Bull Inn

wealthier citizens of Dover moved up the valley and this encouraged the Council to extend the boundaries, taking in Charlton and parts of Buckland. There was another boundary revision in 1851 which took in most of the rest of Buckland and another in 1896.

Mr Bavington-Jones in his book on Dover asserted that there were few houses between the *Eagle Tavern* (more recently the *Irish Times,* now closed) and the *Cherry Tree Inn* at the start of the 19th century, but there do seem to have been some old properties on the right as you climb Buckland Hill, after passing the Charlton Toll Gate. I should point out that the Toll Gate was on the opposite side to the *Eagle Inn* and was removed in 1855 because it created a bottleneck on the London Road. Buckland Hill is the stretch from Beaconsfield Road to the Drill Hall, which is apparent when you come up from the town with a load of shopping!

St. Bartholomew's Hospital
The ground to the west, which until the Dissolution was part of St. Bartholomew's Leper Hospital, did not appear to have been used for housing until about 1825. The situation changed when much of it came on the market after William Kingsford, the miller, was adjudged bankrupt in 1834. This was rising ground to the west leading to Chapel Mount, or the High Meadows where we used to fly our home-made kites. The Buckland boundary was just before the high terrace and can be pin-pointed by the property known as Buckland Place. It is interesting to note that from here up to the *Gate Inn* the road was known as Buckland Street until about 1880 when it became London Road.

Buckland Bottom
Most of the villagers lived near the main road, with farms on the outskirts at Barton and Coombe. The last-mentioned farm, which was in Buckland Bottom, disappeared when it was overtaken by the extension of the rubbish tip. Buckland Bottom in 1807 was the venue for Dover Races and later, in 1835, the place where they built the Buckland Union which was then way out of town.

Gate Inn and toll gate, Crabble Hill, 1869

Buckland Terrace and Methodist Church

Buckland Terrace

In the 1841 Census we can trace Anthony Freeman Payn who was in charge of the well-known York Hotel on the seafront. This stood near the present Clock Tower not far from the swingbridge, and was demolished in 1847 to make way for harbour improvements. The 1851 Census shows him living in York House just in Buckland at the start of the terrace. He died in London in 1866 and was brought back to Buckland for burial. York House still stands. The varied collection of houses on the terrace began to appear about 1840, when plots were sold off.

Buckland Methodists

A little further up the terrace is the Buckland Methodist Chapel with the impressive facade which was built in 1839, strangely it cost £1839. After the Second World War it was closed as a church and used by the Sea Cadets and later became a bingo hall. It has now been restored and renamed King's Hall – the name of an old cinema in Biggin Street. Opposite this chapel in London Road was another Methodist meeting place dating from 1810. I remember Charlie Ashdown running the Happy Hour for children there before 1939 and recall him dishing out aniseed balls as he rode by on his bike; it was said he bought them by the hundredweight! There is still a Methodist church on the corner of Beaconsfield and London Roads dating from early in the twentieth century, but it is not quite in Buckland! John Wesley first established a Methodist society in Dover on his first visit in 1765. In his journal he wrote, 'I preached at noon in Dover to a very serious but small congregation. We afterwards walked to the Castle, on the top of a mountain.'

Buckland Wall

I found an entry in the *Dover Express* of 1894 to say that William Pritchard aged eight died after a fall from Buckland Wall steps, near the chapel. The account reminded its readers that for over 50 years there had been no fence or railings to the steps. Public opinion forced the Corporation to take some action, although the owners were under an obligation to maintain the road and wall. It eventually came before the magistrates for a decision and, from evidence given by the Town Clerk, William Knocker, it was noted that the purchasers had a duty to build the wall to tidy things up when the chalk bank was cut back. It seems that the road was much narrower and could have been treacherous when heavy rains washed down soil from the hills.

Cinemas
Further up the road, on the right, where now there is a car and van hire centre, there was a house known as Bucklands, owned by the Fielding family. On the opposite side of the road there is a gap between the houses, which was at one time laid out as gardens to give a

'Bucklands' about 1900

Old 'Regent' cinema replaced in 1936

Pear Tree Cottages

pleasant view. The Fieldings were unlikely to have approved of the arrival of the Buckland Picture House there in 1920 which was later known as the Regent. In 1936 the bank was removed and a new Regent appeared alongside our old favourite. Later it was renamed the Odeon, but now we have the Territorial Drill Hall in its place.

Cherries and pears

A little further up we have the *Cherry Tree Inn* which shows up in a Licensing List of 1740. It has the distinction of being the first house in the parish to be lit by gas (in 1847). Just beyond Cherry Tree Avenue (formerly Lane) we find the remains of Pear Tree Cottages and incised on a brick we have the date of 1754. There was an old Buckland family by the name of Robbins. They owned the forge from about 1650 to the 1880s that used to be in London Road near Buckland Bridge. Living in Pear Tree Cottages we find Thomas Robbins, who was one of the local blacksmiths. There were others who plied the trades of brassfounders, carpenters and watch-makers. Some of the family moved down-town, but came back to Buckland to be buried, including Jacob who was at one time a victualler in Snargate Street. I have now found members of the family living not far from me who are proud to be Bucklanders.

Buckland Flour Mill

As we continue up the road we pass the white-boarded flour mill built by William Kingsford in 1812. There was another mill on the other side of the River Dour which had been making paper since 1795 and later became Hardings Brewery. Later still it was Wellington's Brewery. To reach this site today you cross over the bridge in Lorne Road, built by William in 1815 as a stone in the arch signifies.

Buckland Flour Mill – Mannerings formerly Kingsfords

Wellington Brewery in the foreground with Kingsford's Buckland Paper Mill and Brewery in the background. Photograph by G. Amos about 1880

Lundy House

Lundy House

In 1820, William Kingsford built as his residence, next door to his mill, Lundy House, which is still there. He probably lived there until he went bankrupt in 1834. On the roof of Lundy House there was a platform on which was mounted a telescope. I understand that a member of the Mannering family, who later owned the mill and the house, was fond of star-gazing. The Mannering family ran the mill until it closed in 1958. I remember that the trams always made a special stop to pick up Edward Mannering outside his house and the tram crews, about 40 people in all, always received a Christmas box of half a crown each from him!

The Kingsfords

The Kingsford family were associated with this area for nearly two hundred years. I have not been too sure about the relationships between the Kingsfords, but I am inclined to think that they came to Dover in the early 1800s possibly from Canterbury. The first mention I can find of a Kingsford in the Freemen's Rolls is Edward, who purchased his freedom for £20 in 1802. This buying of a freedom usually indicates someone coming into the town to set up in business. Pigot's 1823 Directory lists Edward Kingsford at Archcliffe Brewery. William Kingsford the elder, having bought the lands of the medieval leper hospital of St Bartholomew in about 1810, then carried on business in Buckland. My great-grandfather was a miller following in his father's footsteps and they both lived in a cottage belonging to William Kingsford near the Buckland Flour Mill. My grandfather had a brother, Kingsford Harman who was probably named after Mr Kingsford.

Windmill Brewery

Windmill Brewery stood at the corner of London Road and Coombe Valley Road and many must have passed by the site, now occupied by Kingsford Court, without realising its

Kingsford's Windmill Brewery, 1847

interesting history. According to Bavington-Jones in his book on Dover written in 1907, it was Flavius Ignatious who built it in 1829. We know it was associated with Alfred Kingsford for many years. Pigot's 1826 Directory lists Alfred at Archcliffe Fort Brewery and in 1832 he is shown as being at Buckland Brewery. He had two sons, one Flavius and the other Cottenham, who ran the business in later years. They were both town councillors in 1879. The 1861 Census shows Alfred living in Lundy House, and earlier we find him in Ivy House which backed on to the Windmill Brewery. The house still stands although bereft of its ivy.

Amos' photograph of Buckland windmill and brewery with brickfield (now Magdala Road) in foreground, about 1865

Windmill

The windmill incorporated in the brewery could have been one built at Buckland in 1798. It was built by a millwright as a model for what he could produce and it did grind corn for a while, but was then used for pumping water. This could have been a factor in siting the brewery on this spot, and, from reports, the well water in this area had a peculiar iron or chalybeate quality. Sir Thomas Hyde Page owned the St. Bartholomew lands and sold them to William Kingsford after he left Dover in 1804. At that time there was no road leading up through Buckland Bottom. It was not until the Union was built that Union Road, now Coombe Valley Road, came into being.

Palmer's Coachworks

The brewery seems to have been still operating in 1881 but in 1887 George Beer and Rigden took it over and by 1889 it had stopped brewing. By 1896 Palmer's Connaught Coachworks had moved in. Palmers were wheel-wrights and coach builders in Dover from 1875 with workshops in Priory Street and, then from around 1896, on the site of Kingsford's Windmill Brewery and at their Cherry Tree Avenue workshops, now the Aldi supermarket. By 1909 G.S. Palmer & Son employed over 100 staff. George Palmer's son was in the Dover Camera Club with me years later. My Uncle Ernie worked there as a carpenter as did Graham Tutthill's grandfather (Graham is Chief Reporter, Dover Mercury). Chassis were bought in and then Palmers craftsmen built bodies to order including Rolls Royces and some East Kent buses. Chassis were often driven from Cherry Tree to the Windmill Brewery site by drivers sitting on a temporary wooden seat. Finished cars were often towed to Dover Priory Station by horse en route to London and elsewhere.

G.S. Palmer, Coachbuilder, 1908

This business survived until the beginning of the Second World War when Jenkins and Pain, motor body repairers, moved onto the site from Limekiln Street. About ten years ago they moved out, the site was sold and the old brewery buildings demolished to make way for the aptly named Kingsford Court.

Demolition of the brewery

During demolition a brick was found in a flint wall with the initials of T.H.P. carved in it, and as this was in a boundary wall it could have connections with a Mr T. Paul who lived in Grove House (now the site of Charles Lister Court) close by. It is difficult to be sure when the windmill was taken down but the boundary wall is still in position and with the assistance of neighbours in Magdala Road I found a stone in one of the buttresses with the name of *A. KINGSFORD* inscribed but the date below had been eroded.

While talking to the demolition team they told me that a bottle had been found. On investigation it turned out to be a Codds bottle complete with marble stopper. This had the name 'Forster's Chemists Dover' who had a ginger beer factory and were listed in Castle Street from the 1880s. I began to despair of finding evidence of bottling, but one of the workmen said they had found some labels when floor timbers were raised. They apparently were the type put over the stoppers and had the name of Kingsford printed on them. One of the photographs taken by W.H. Boyer of Sandwich (1868-1897) shows the *New Inn* at Sandwich with a board advertising 'Kingsford's Dover Fine Ales'. Perhaps someone might be able to supply the family history of the Kingsfords and there may be a collector who has one of their bottles.

Providence Place

Still walking up London Road, on the right beyond Lundy House we come to five flint cottages once known as Providence Place. There was a tablet, dated 1836, at the rear which has begun to weather away but I was able to decipher most of it,

'That he be dead, He is not forgot,
by him that had, these letters wrote'.

This ground was sold off, according to a sales notice, in 1834, which indicated that my great-great-grandfather was living in a cottage there at the time of W. Kingsford's bankruptcy.

White's, the fruit and vegetable shop, was here until it closed during 2000 when Alfie White retired after more than half a century selling fruit and vegetables. He took over his parents' shop which they started in 1945. The premises had previously been Clark's the butcher, a slaughterhouse and a dairy.

Old Endeavour

On the same side of the street is the *Old Endeavour* pub. There were several pubs with this name locally – in Bulwark Street, River and Wootton – and you might guess that they were named after Captain Cook's ship, but I think it more likely that they were named after a privateer called *Endeavour* built in Dover and licensed by the Crown to harass the French during the Napoleonic Wars. The present inn sign is a painting of Captain Cook's ship.

A Mr East is shown as the landlord in the 1841 census, but there must have been some sort of dispute because by the 1871 census he had moved to the *New Endeavour* just a few doors up (which is now a second-hand furniture shop) where two cottages had been knocked into one and converted to an inn.

Girls of Buckland School, 1901

Captain Cockburn's painting of Buckland Bridge and Church, 1837

Buckland Farm Lodge, 1937, by the tram sheds

Buckland Bridge

We continue towards Buckland Bridge and pass the old school on our left, built in 1852 for £842. When digging out the foundations builders found Roman pottery and also much tufa. The latter is found in old river beds and was used as a building material. From this we can infer that the river was much wider at one time. In 1901 there were about 250 girls at the school and in 1904 there were 389 girls plus 697 infants with some classes using the Rectory garden. A boys' school had been built on the site of Barton Farm in 1898 followed by an infants' school in 1903 which found room for me in 1920.

A little distance up the road is a pair of houses which used to have bricks with the date 1808 and various initials. These may have had some connection with local brick-makers, who abounded in this area. It seems possible that this was the *Chequers Beer House* kept by Richard Pay the shoemaker according to the 1841 Census. Door sills show signs of being hollowed out by barrels being dragged through. As we cross over Buckland Bridge we see the old tram shed, built in 1897 and now a motor showroom. I reported there just over 60 years ago for my first job. On our left is Buckland Paper Mill which was closed in 2000. This old-established industry may go back to 1638 on this site when Thomas Chapman, a papermaker, was married at Buckland.

Crabble Hill

Going up Crabble Hill we reach the *Three Cups*, opposite which was the Old Toll Gate House. After the end of the Turnpike in 1866 the Corporation used it for collecting the coal dues on coal arriving by rail and road. One of the older policemen was used for this job, and there is an entry in the burial records that PC Charles Judge Stevens lost his 16 years old daughter in 1889 from consumption. There was a note that the River Dour ran at the back of his garden.

Saxon burial ground

In 1951 I heard they were digging on the hill close to Green Lane and decided to have a look on the way home from work. They were preparing the ground for new council houses, and the bulldozers had turned up some bones and other items. Fortunately someone moved quickly and Miss Vera Evison was sent down to organise a rescue dig. I arrived just as it was getting dark and helped to put the cover over one of the graves, nearly putting my foot in it in the process. After 20 years, I thought I would enquire at our local museum as to what had been found. I was given Miss Evison's address at Birkbeck College and wrote to her. She gave me some information, but suggested that I write to the British Museum and ask to see the finds. A date was arranged, I took a day off, caught the train and spent an hour in a room at the British Museum examining the artefacts and handling one of the swords. Shortly after that some of the items went on display, and I believe it is still possible to see them. Some items are now in Dover Museum. A full report was eventually published and there is a copy in Dover Reference Library.

The burial ground would seem to indicate that Saxon invaders sailed up the valley and established a settlement at Buckland after the Roman Legions had left or were they already here as mercenary troops? It is as well to recall that the River Dour was much wider and more navigable in Roman times, and continued so until the Norman period when the estuary began to silt-up. I can visualise their longboats drawn up on the river bank, and

Buckland Church with the paper mill in the background

perhaps only a stone's throw from where I live at the bottom of St Radigund's Road. A find was made there which is linked with the graves. The grave goods indicate that they belonged to warriors and the site was in use intermittently from about 475 until 800 A.D. I have sat up on the hill near the cemetery site and, looking down to the sea, tried to imagine what the valley below looked like some 1500 years ago.

St. Andrew's Church
It would be wrong to leave out St. Andrew's Church which is the oldest building in the parish, and appears to have some Saxon work in its fabric. I wonder if the first church was built by the descendants of those warriors up on the hill? We now have a daughter church up near those graves which is dedicated to St. Nicholas and that may be a link with those Saxon seafarers. Back in 1880 they moved the old yew tree to make it possible to extend the Church of St. Andrew, and many Bucklanders have a small wooden cross made by Mr Yarrow (a craftsman who worked for Mr Thomas, a local ironmonger) from a branch which broke off in a storm.

I think that I have proved my point that there is still plenty of evidence of Buckland's interesting past.

Chapter 10

PAPER MILLS OF THE DOUR

The end of Buckland Paper Mill
It was not a happy day when I was taken round the Buckland Paper Mill for the last time before it closed during 2000 and production was switched to the Aberdeen mill of Arjo Wiggins. No doubt this was the end of paper making on the River Dour after hundreds of years. It struck me how few staff are required to run a mill with all the modern technology and I cast my mind back to the day when I started work at the tramshed opposite the mill in 1929. I can still see the many men and girls clocking on underneath the clock tower.

Papermaking
Paper used to be made from a well-soaked mixture of rags and wood fibre called stuff which was boiled, pounded by hammers and stirred. It was then scooped up in a deckel (tray), shaken left and right, backwards and forwards to spread the fibres. When the water drained away, the residue had to be dried either by tipping it onto felt or by hanging it in the loft of the paper mill supported by horsehair or cowgut which did not leave a mark. It was heated from underneath which sometimes resulted in fire! This made brown paper. To make it white the paper had to be bleached, creating a terrible smell. It was all a very fine art, especially judging the right quantities of rags, starch etc. Now it is not only made by machine but computerised too!

Six paper mills
As well as several corn mills, there have been six mills making paper on the Dour: Bushy Ruff, River, Crabble, Buckland, Lower Buckland and Charlton. All but Charlton relied on

Buckland Paper Mill about 1936

water power; Bushy Ruff Mill survived on water rising in the Alkham Valley until about 1860.

The Battle of Bushy Ruff

The name Bushy Ruff (or Bushy Rough, the names seem to be interchangeable) goes back many years, but the colonial style house was built about 1825 for William Knocker, a mayor of Dover. Previously, in 1795, he had built a paper mill (near the lodge house by the present Alkham Road. This caused problems later because the old road ran where the waterwheel was placed.

Today's road from Alkham, when it reaches Bushy Ruff, bends to the south of Bushy Ruff Lake, but before 1795 it continued straight on, passing the Lake on the north side. Following the building of the mill, it was easier for traffic to take a route south of the Lake through what was Coxhill Farm. Justices' Minutes 1855 to 1859 reveal court cases arising from this practice!

When Mrs Charlotte Every became the owner of Coxhill Farm in 1856 she gave instructions to her agent for the new road to be blocked. Soon there was a confrontation. After Alkham folk had passed through on their way to Dover market a four feet wide trench was dug across the road between Kearsney Abbey and Bushy Ruff. The Highway Surveyor gave instructions for the work to stop without success. It is not recorded what the Alkham folk did upon their return faced with a five mile detour!

The agent was taken to court by the Parish of River and was convicted, but the trench remained. Alkham Parish then sent Mr Collard and two worthies to fill it in. Nearly finished, the agent arrived and ordered them off. Mr Collard stood his ground and took the agent to court for assault. Again he was convicted and was fined 1/- plus costs.

Not to be defeated, the agent then placed a barrier across the new road. An Alkham stalwart Valentine Gambrill, arrived and attempted to climb over. The agent tried to remove him but was struck with a walking stick. Taken to court, Mr Gambrill was fined 1/- plus costs for taking matters into his own hands!

Mr Collard then took the Highways Surveyor to court for failing to carry out his duties. The court ruled that the road was a highway and that the surveyor was bound to keep it free of obstruction. He was also fined 1/- plus costs!

So ended the 'Battle of Bushy Ruff'. Over the years I recall at least two occasions when the gate at the Alkham end of Bushy Ruff has been damaged by unknown vehicles. I wonder if it was the ghost of Mrs Every trying to drive a coach and horses through to re-establish the old highway!

Plan of Bushy Ruff Paper Mill built 1825

River Paper Mill around 1900

River Paper Mill ruins today

River and Crabble Mills

Papermaking at River Mill is first mentioned in 1689. William Phipps, a young journeyman papermaker, bought River Mill with John Aldridge in 1780. In 1790 William Phipps built Crabble Paper Mill (on the corner of Crabble Road and Lower Road) and had connections with Lower Buckland Mill. Until 1803 all paper was made by hand in single sheets. One of the first papermaking machines in England was installed at Crabble in 1807. The machine was driven by a water wheel and had no dryers with the paper being removed by hand and loft-dried. William's sons, Christopher and John, who carried on the business, patented the dandy roll in 1825 – a wooden roller covered with wire mesh to which the watermark was attached – which gave the paper a watermark. Following the deaths of John and Christopher Phipps, their nephew, Filmer Phipps, ran both River and Crabble Paper Mills. River Mill continued to make paper until 1918. The ruins of this mill can still be seen at the bottom of Minnis Lane with the Dour cascading over them where children have great fun.

Crabble Mill was closed down in 1894 but was bought by Wiggins Teape in 1895 and converted into a rag preparation plant for Buckland Mill. Unfortunately, it was burnt down in 1906. I understand that a dining room and recreation hall were provided in gratitude for the efforts made by the workers to save the mill. It was soon rebuilt and 200 people mainly female worked there. Much later in 1947, the rag preparation was moved to Buckland and I still remember the terrible smell when I walked through Church Alley beside the mill. Sorting the rags was hard work. Only cotton rags were used and anything not cotton had to be cut off – buttons, elastic etc. It was hard work and the women, who were called 'rag dollies' were quite a tough bunch – woebetide any man who walked through the works unprotected!

Crabble Paper Mill fire, 1906

Crabble Mill Rag Dollies, 1900

Above: Dandy Roll
Left: Rags ready for pulping

Buckland Paper Mill, 1770

Buckland Paper Mill

Buckland Paper Mill appears in a painting of 1770. However, there is mention of papermaking at Buckland in 1638 when Thomas Chapman, a paper-maker, was married at Buckland and in 1705 another papermaker was also married in the parish. The Horns bought Buckland Mill from the Archbishop of Canterbury in 1788 having leased it since 1746. The papermaking of the Horn family was more of a cottage industry in the 18th century. Sometime in the 1790s there was a fire and then the mill was enlarged. On the 6th January 1814 the mill was burnt down again due to sheets of paper falling on to the stove in the drying room. Thomas Pattenden in his diary records that Mr. Horn's dwelling house was also destroyed. The rebuilt mill was still operated by water-power with no papermaking machine, unlike Crabble Mill. Buckland House on Crabble Hill was built in 1823 by Thomas Horne's son Thomas.

Lower Buckland Mill

Lower Buckland Mill, does not seem to have made paper until 1775 when a deed mentions a newly erected paper mill. I have an indenture dated 1829 with a Kingsford watermark; William Kingsford owned the mill at that time. The papermaking buildings were upstream from Lorne Road on the other side of the river from Kingsford's Corn Mill (later Mannering's Mill which still survives as a building on the corner of Lorne and London Roads). Following Kingsford's bankruptcy the paper mill was sold in 1834 and in 1847 it was converted into a brewery, known first as Harding's and later as the Wellington Brewery.

George Dickinson

George Dickinson bought Buckland Mill from Thomas Horn in 1822 and Bushy Rough Mill in 1826. About 1833 he built a steam paper mill at Charlton off Peter Street, which was later known as Spring Garden Paper Mill. His mother provided him with financial backing. He ordered two machines and one was placed in Buckland Mill, which was the end of hand-made paper there. He wanted to get rich quick but he overstretched himself and became bankrupt in 1837. In 1838 Buckland Mill was offered for sale with a seventeen foot diameter wheel, four engines and three machines, a steam boiler and a drying room. The latter was 140 feet long and there was a bleaching room which meant that white paper was being produced. The machine put in by George was not listed, and his failure was almost certainly due to his Charlton Mill venture. Buckland Mill seems to have been unoccupied for several years after the bankruptcy. George died in 1843.

It was he who built as a house for himself the building we now know as the old Victoria Hospital; he called it Brook House – not to be confused with the other, later, Brook House now demolished.

The Weatherbys and Ashdowns
The Weatherby family appear for a while as lessees of Buckland Mill. Charles Ashdown arrived in 1849 and had some sort of rental agreement until about 1851. Then Chartham Mill which was owned by the Weatherbys was burnt down and the Weatherbys seemed to disappear from the Buckland scene. Charles Ashdown carried on. Up to 1879 water power was enough to drive the mill but then two steam engines were installed. Following the death of Charles Ashdown in 1877, his son, Charles, who had little papermaking expertise, offered Henry Hobday, manager at Snodland Mill, a partnership in 1879 .

Henry was born at Chartham in 1838 soon after his father, Daniel, moved to that paper mill. Chartham Mill was burnt down in 1850 and was rebuilt with a machine. Daniel 'turned out' with others who were opposed to machines, but later returned to Chartham. He was a regular churchgoer and stood up during the sermon after a 24 hour shift so that he did not fall asleep!

Wiggins Teape, Edward Barlow and the Hobdays
A disastrous fire in 1887 practically destroyed Buckland Mill. The papermaking machine with its 70 skeletal reels was a pitiful wreck; however, it was rebuilt in 1888. In the same year Henry Hobday, after some hesitation, took on the contract to make Conqueror paper for Mr Edward Barlow, a director of Wiggins Teape, in order to keep the mill running. It

1887 Fire

was at a rather low price, 3¾d. per pound, but he thought he would take a chance. Conqueror paper was to become the best known watermarked paper in the world! Ashdown and Hobday had lost business due to the fire and they struggled on until 1890 when they accepted an offer of £20,000 from Wiggins Teape & Co., Henry Hobday stayed on to run the mill. The Board of Directors under Mr. Edward Barlow decided to install another machine and bought one from Hollingbourne which was under used due to lack of sufficient water. Henry Hobday's son, Lewis, now seventeen, was sent to dismantle it with the assistance of an elderly millwright and two labourers. They managed the job in nine weeks and the sections were shipped by rail and then road drawn by traction engines. No. 2 machine was duly installed at Buckland in 1893. Production rose to 800 tons per annum – later it was to rise to 70 tons per week!

However, in 1894 when they were starting it up they had problems. They had increased the steam pressure and installed new piping when a pipe burst which badly scalded a workman and blew Lewis Hobday off the scaffolding causing facial burns which put him off work for three months.

Demand increased and a third machine was needed, but first they looked round for a mill that could take some of the work. Frank Barlow and Lewis Hobday were sent up to Cathcart Mill near Glasgow which was idle, but the water supply was contaminated by its peaty nature and the quality of the paper produced was not good. Eventually, this was resolved by installing a Bells water filter. Lewis travelled up and down to Cathcart until the problem was resolved.

I knew Lewis Hobday quite well due to his connection with the Scout Movement, and his brother, Maurice, with whom I became quite friendly in later years. Lewis lived quite close to my house in St. Radigund's Road for a number of years. Lewis took over from his father in 1906.

Mr E.P. Barlow was very keen to make photographic paper with the assistance of Rajah

Buckland Bridge, 1894, before the house was demolished to extend the Mill

Buckland Mill No.3 machine, 1928

Ltd. but without much success at first. Lewis had a small laboratory under the clock tower and had some assistance from a chemist. Buckland was too busy to run test runs and the work was transferred to Chafford Mill at Fordcombe near Tunbridge Wells. The war of 1914-18 stopped imports of photographic paper and the government gave permission to build a new mill in Buckinghamshire to manufacture it which was successful.

In 1910 the Board decided to install a third machine at Buckland. It was designed and installed by Lewis and his brother John at a cost of over £50,000. The machine was started up in July 1911 and ran well in spite of some sloppy belts. The machine was designed to produce 40 tons of ledger papers in a five and half day week, but this was doubled in a short time.

Having built Kearsney Court in the Alkham Valley Road as his new home, E.P. Barlow died in 1912 and Lewis felt his loss very deeply. Lewis had taken over from his father as manager and had moved into Buckland House on Crabble Hill.

Wars and depression
The 1914-18 war caused problems as there was a shortage of labour due to conscription. Cutter boys were moved to man the papermaking machines and women from the rag preparation plant took on their jobs. The labour shortage later became so acute that it was necessary to close down No. 1 machine. During the war the mill was making Admiralty chart papers and also Army map papers plus tracing papers. After the war trade picked up but by 1921, due to the depression, there was short time working at the mill. During 1923 to 1930 Wiggins Teape took over 12 mills after it became a public company; Lewis was

involved in the reorganisation. He retired in 1934 and was asked to go out to St.Helena to restart a mill and was out there for two years.

The mill continued to work during the Second World War until a Spitfire crashed on to the roof above No. 3 machine. I actually saw the aircraft coming down like a falling leaf, and the pilot landed by parachute not far away. As he was a Pole, he was mistaken for a German and was met by the local ladies with their carving knives at the ready. Thankfully, someone assured them he was one of ours. The mill was closed down as shelling had started and staff were transferred; some moved down to Hampshire.

Post war
The mill reopened in 1945. Crabble Mill became a storage depot replaced by a new rag house on the Buckland site in 1947. In 1953 No. 1 machine was given over to making plastic based papers for Formica. Production was rising and the salle was completely reorganised – the salle was a long building where the female staff sorted and counted the sheets of paper, removing dirty and creased sheets for repulping. In 1956, the old steam boiler house with its six hand-fired Lancashire boilers was replaced by a grate feed water tube boiler. In 1994 the Combined Heat and Power Plant was commissioned which meant a change from coal to natural gas; this was able to supply the mill and Dover Harbour Board with electricity. With the closing down of Buckland Mill and no demand for steam this plant has also closed. Now this ancient paper making site awaits its new future.

Buckland Mill Salle, 1928

Footnote I should like to clear up some confusion caused by an entry in the book *Perambulation of Dover* written by John Bavington-Jones in which he states that it was William Rastall Dickenson who built Charlton Paper Mill; but he was misinformed as it was George Dickinson, whom we have already found at Buckland. This is confirmed by C.P. Davies, a noted historian. Confusion might have been caused by Mr Rastall Dickenson who married Mr Fector's daughter. Mr Fector was a local banker who was involved in George Dickinson's financial dealings.

Chapter 11

EARLY FIRE SERVICES

While searching through the Dover Paving Commission Minutes (1788-1838) I came across items dealing with firefighting and it reminded me that the Chamberlain's Accounts also included similar entries. In early times most buildings were of wood and so were very vulnerable to fire, especially those with thatched roofs. There is evidence of fires during the Saxon period and we know William I destroyed the town by fire. In those days it was difficult to put out a fire and it was often only possible to tear off the burning thatch and endeavour to prevent it spreading. They then seemed to have rebuilt and covered the ashes with crushed chalk.

In 1702 there is an item in the Chamberlain's books of the payment of 6d. for 'Carridge of the Town Fire Hooke'. However in 1700 the Mayor Edward Wivell had presented the town with a fire engine. In 1735 12s. was paid for trying the fire engine and in 1742 John Longley was paid 14/- for 'Oyling ye Engine and Pipes'. In 1785 there is an entry for proving the engine. Next year we find that the porters were paid for exercising the engine, and in 1788 examining and trying it out. On November 5th in the same year, 'Paid men for carrying buckets at a fire 2s.0d.' This was one of the Days of Rejoicing and the porters had to construct the bonfire, while John Children (saddler) was paid for repairing the fire engine pipes and buckets. The leather had to be kept pliable possibly with neatsfoot oil.

The minutes of the Paving Commission in 1824 'Ordered that it is part of the duty of the porters appointed by the Board to practise and exercise the Fire Engines in order that they may always be in working condition. The porters shall be summoned by the Town Sergeant on the first Monday in every two months to assemble at the Hole in the Wall at a certain hour to be appointed. Ten shillings a time to be expended on beer.' The Hole in the Wall was not a hostelry but one of the town's gates. The *Britannia Inn* stands almost on that site. It seems that the porters were to be as well oiled as the engines. Due to the passing of the Third Paving Act the Corporation transferred the fire engines to the Commission.

Fire Engine Committee
Regulations were made by the Fire Engine Committee and they included the instruction that the watchmen should give the alarm: 'The Church, Harbour, Town and Ordnance bells to be rung. The keys of the engine house to be kept by the gaoler. The porters to have the number of their engine inscribed on their ticket, and horses to be obtained from Mr Grant if required.' Five guineas was to be paid to the crew of the first engine on the scene.

The Fire Station seems to have been in Queen Street as there seems to have been some connection with the Old Gaol. A list was compiled showing the manning of the engines. The foreman of No. 1 Engine was John Marsh, the Mayor's Sergeant, with eleven ticket porters. No. 2 Engine was under the command of the Town Crier, Thomas C. Marsh. Two engines are seen at work in the picture of the fire in Snargate Street in 1837.

Fire! Fire!

In 1834 the *Dover Telegraph* reported a fire in Grubbins Lane at a storehouse of Mr Page the grocer. A bucket chain was formed by troops and with the assistance of three females standing in the Dour these buckets were refilled. The report added that it was fortunate that the tide was running and so there was a good supply of water. The route would have been up Fishmongers Lane across Bench Street to the lane now known as Chapel Lane. The Fire Engine Committee met in 1838 and agreed that part of the Town Pound be appropriated as an Engine House to be converted at the expense of the Commission, and also that boards be put up in the streets to indicate fire plugs.

Job for the police

In 1836 the Police Force had been transferred to the new Corporation, and they became responsible for manning the fire engines. The 1841 Census shows a superintendent and eleven constables in Queen Street. The police stayed there until they moved to the basement of the Maison Dieu in 1881. The fire engines remained until they moved

1837 Snargate Street fire captured by W. Heath

to Ladywell fifty years later. Two policemen continued to live there and were available to man the engine. There was an item in the *Dover Chronicle* of May 28th 1870 which reported the discussion on providing a telegraph link between the police station and waterworks at Connaught Hill. At certain times the mains were not charged due to loss of water through leaks. This meant it was necessary to send a runner up to the waterworks to get a supply to the hydrants. The cost would have been £78, and one councillor thought the insurance companies should pay. In any case his houses were well insured and they would have to pay out more if there was a delay.

We know that during 1887 and 1888 the fire waggon and fire escape were lodged in part of the covered market. Mr W.H. Wright who had bought the right to collect market tolls submitted an account to the Mayor and Corporation claiming rent for them at £2 a month. 'Hire of Market 14 Months October 1887-December 1888 £28.' Mr Wright again was successful in his bid for the toll rights for three years from 1890, but there is no evidence that the mayor paid the rent.

In 1899 Dover had a new horse-drawn fire engine with a Merryweather pump. This

1899 Merryweather fire engine about 1910

continued until 1922 with Mr Nash supplying the horses. These were trotted down the main street while the fireman was igniting the fire under the steam boiler of the engine. Dover had hose reel stations in various parts of the town, and the police pushed or pulled the curricle with standpipe and hoses etc aboard. In most cases they were able to plug into a convenient hydrant and deal with the fire. From newspaper reports it would seem that the engine was seldom turned out due to the time factor. The story is told of one policeman who took hold of the shafts of the two-wheeled curricle and started off to a fire in the Pier District. His colleagues were supposed to push or hold back as the case may be. He was descending the slope of the viaduct and they failed to hang on. The curricle gathered speed and he was forced to run faster and faster to avoid being flattened by the weighty vehicle behind him. Fortunately he reached level ground before collapsing, never having been so scared before in his life.

Motorised fire engines

I had some difficulty in finding the date when Dover had its first motor fire engine. On February 17th 1922 there was a report in the *Dover Express* of a fire at Farthingloe Farm and the Dover engine was requested to attend, but there was a delay in obtaining horses from Mr Nash. He may have been providing transport for a funeral and I know that he supplied a cab to transport my sister and me to the Isolation Hospital when we contracted diphtheria in January of that year. However, they did reach the scene just before the Folkestone motor fire waggon. As you can guess there was a letter in the next edition suggesting it was about time we had a motorised fire appliance. The comment from the *Express* was that Dover should not have to foot the bill for out of town fires, as the curricles could cope with fires in the borough. In the issue of 31st March the Watch Committee were discussing buying a second-hand army lorry and fitting it up with a

Merryweather pump. It was noted that the lorry would cost £337 and Merryweathers wanted £960 for fitting the pump. In that same year on September 2nd there was a fire at Martin and the new Dover fire engine attended with Inspector Fleet in charge. Over a thousand feet of hose was used to bring water from the waterworks. This engine was a Peerless chain driven with solid tyres and was named 'Margaret' after the Mayoress, the wife of Mr R.J. Barwick, a local builder. There was an escape ladder kept in Gaol Lane which at night was wheeled round to the Market Square and chained to a lamp post. Later 'Margaret' was provided with supports.

King's Hall Cinema fire, 1937, with 'Rosetta' Leyland fire engine fitted with Metz turntable ladder in Queen's Gardens

In 1930 we saw the arrival of 'Ellen', a Morris named after the wife of the Mayor, Alderman Russell. In March 1931 this engine was called to a fire in Tower Hamlets Street and the onlookers were surprised to see the firemen with black faces until they remembered that the Police Nigger Minstrel Troupe was performing at the Town Hall! December 1931 saw the opening of the new fire station in Ladywell and 'Margaret' and 'Ellen' were on view. I can remember the Mayor opening it and the doors being flung back by the pull of a cord.

1930 Morris fire engine 'Ellen' in Union Road, 1938

In May 1937 we had a new Leyland fire engine, named 'Rosetta' after Mayor Norman's wife, with a Metz turntable ladder, which I believe the Chief Constable Marshall Bolt had pressed for. On December 29th of that year we had the fire at the King's Hall Cinema in which this new equipment played its part. I was down there next morning with a crowd at the end of Queens Gardens which was roped off. The only person who was allowed in was a baker from Holmes Morris which was still able to operate as a bakery. The Police Fire Brigade managed to contain the fire thanks to 'Rosetta'; its 104 feet extension ladder made it possible to direct the water from above and I am told that PC Punter, our tallest policeman, was directing the jet. The film being shown was *Oh, Mr Porter* with Will Hay. I am afraid the old ticket porters would have found it hard work, and it was appropriate that the 1837 picture of them was published with pictures of the fire. They did start to rebuild the cinema but the war intervened.

Auxiliary Fire Service

I joined the Auxiliary Fire Service when it was formed in 1938. In Dover we had four Coventry Climax trailer pumps and one larger pump on a four wheeled trailer. At the time of the Munich Crisis I was just going on holiday to Shropshire – my first good holiday. Instead, I thought I had better go and volunteer for something, so I went to the police and they gave me all sorts of jobs. One of them was to go out to River after they had sounded the old siren at Buckland Paper Mill at noon to see if anybody had heard it – nobody had! They were dishing out gas masks at River School.

Next day I thought I had better go round and help out the Fire Service. I well remember riding round the town on 'Rosetta' with Sergeant McLeod assessing our resources! We went round to see what pumps we had available in case of incendiary bombs. It was pathetic – virtually nothing. On 4th February 1939 we had a black-out exercise. I was picked as engineer on No. 2 Patrol and we had a call to the seafront near the old seaplane sheds. Equipment was still short and the standpipe was a little unusual. The order was given for water on and I slowly opened the water valve but the cry was, 'Nothing coming through,' from the branchman, 'Block' Wood. I then remembered that odd piece on the standpipe and, finding it in the dark, I pushed it. Then there was a shout and I realised the hose had whipped as water went through and my friend had nearly lost his hold. It was some time before he would accept my explanation.

AFS trailer pump in Dover Carnival, 1938

Joe in the Auxiliary Fire Service, 1939

On September 3rd 1939 when the siren sounded I was at a service in Charlton Church. I ran across the churchyard, leapt over the wall, ran home, donned my uniform and thumbed a lift on a milk float and, with others, reported to the Finnis's Hill sub station but it was a false alarm! Recently I was able to visit this spot, at the back of Hammond's the shipping agents, now overgrown with ivy and the roadway gone. However, I did manage to get into the caves and to see the AFS badge over the entrance and added underneath, 'Snug as a bug in a rug'. I continued part-time until sometime in 1940, assigned to Woodlands in Bridge Street and was on duty during the height of the Battle of Britain. In 1941 the Auxiliary Fire Service became the National Fire Service.

Chapter 12

PHOTOGRAPHERS

I have been a keen amateur photographer since boyhood. My New Romney grandmother bought me my first camera, a Number 2 Box Brownie, as a birthday or Christmas present before I left school at 14. One of the drawbacks of having a birthday so soon after Christmas Day was that I often had a present that would do for both! Then I bought a Scout Camera which was a folding camera that fitted on to your Scout belt. When I was 16 or so and working on the trams I bought a much better camera, a Kodak VPK (Vest Pocket Camera), which I could wear under my tramway uniform. This was very useful because I was ready for action at any time! When I was in the Ambulance Service I earned some very useful extra cash teaching Civil Defence volunteers to drive and treated myself to a German Paxette with interchangeable lenses. Later, I changed again to a Practika. Now I use a simple to use 'hi-tech' Kodak APS with its choice of three sizes of photograph!

Train Ferry Dock
In 1933 not far from the Crosswall terminus of the Dover Trams, a start was made on a large engineering project – the building of the train ferry dock at Western Docks. I had, by then, my Kodak VPK. As our terminus was right outside the Hotel-de-Paris, I asked the landlady, Mrs Cone, if I could go on to the roof to take some pictures.

  One day when I was on late shift I clambered out on to the roof to record the work that had begun on the construction of the dock gates by William Arroll & Co. The resulting

Train ferry dock under construction with Hotel de Paris in background, 1935

Train ferry dock under construction

photos were shown to some of the workmen and they suggested that I should show them to the foreman. I was duly escorted into the presence of Mr Hardgraft, who was delighted and asked me to get some copies done. He knew that the bosses in Glasgow would be interested, as no official photographs had been taken. I was then accepted as the unofficial photographer and was able to wander in and out and add to my collection of pictures of the work in progress. I took groups of the workers and was able to sell postcards at 6d. a time which almost covered the cost of my films!

I made some good friends among the workers and they kept me informed on how the construction was progressing so that I was on hand with my camera to record anything of significance. One day I was warned off by a new overseer, but it was my lucky day, as a short while later one of the 150 feet-long derricks collapsed; I must confess that next day I slipped in to photograph the twisted remains. I continued taking photographs until the day before the Southern Railway took possession and I also managed a shot of the first trucks being shunted on to the *Hampton Ferry* on 28th September 1936. Sadly, when the new train ferry berth was opened in 1988, the old train-ferry dock was filled in. Now it, too, has given way to the second cruise liner terminal.

Radar towers
I had made friends with many of the workers on the train ferry dock project. After it was completed I met up with one of the carpenters and he suggested I went up to the old Swingate Aerodrome to take some photos of his new job. I cycled up and saw that four wooden towers were being built. I took several photos including one looking up inside a tower. At the time the *News Chronicle* national newspaper was running a competition for unusual photographs and I sent the 'inside' shot to the paper. Luckily it was returned unpublished, because I think all hell would have broken loose at the Ministry of Defence! These wooden towers were later replaced by the metal radar towers we know so well.

There were four more of these not far from Canterbury. When I was with the Ambulance Service our radio engineer was erecting an aerial on top of a water tower and had a good view across country towards Dunkirk (Kent, not France) and he could see the towers quite well. After a while he could only count three, then two and as he came down, only one! He really thought he had taken leave of his senses! Later, they discovered that demolition contractors had put charges under the legs which had brought the masts, one by one, crashing to earth.

Camera Club
A man in Boots got me to join the Dover Camera Club when I was in the Scouts – even though I had failed my photographer's badge! Important people were members of the Camera Club – like Mr Loxton, the Town Clerk, and Charlie Chitty, the mill owner. I remember that I received a 'highly commended' for a photo of clouds with the sun behind

'Herald of the Night'

them over Folkestone that I called 'Herald of the Night' – even though I took it underexposed during the day to get the effect! I remember a trip with the Club to Poulton Farm in 1937 when I took a photograph of the stone that marks the spot where Poulton Church, mentioned in Domesday Book, once stood. There was a settlement there before St. Radigund's Abbey was built.

I didn't rejoin after the War, but I sometimes went to meetings at the School of Art in The Paddock when Charlie Chitty showed his slides. On one occasion the caretaker wanted to lock up, but Charlie wanted to go on, so the caretaker turned the power off!

Dover's photographers
I have always had an interest in the development of the art and in those enterprising men who set up in business as photographers in towns like Dover. When that well-known local photographer Ray Warner died it made me realise that we were at the end of an era,

especially in portrait photography and it was time to take stock of Dover's photographers over the years, as revealed by directories, newspaper advertisements and other records.

Camera obscura

The story begins earlier than you might think in the closing years of the eighteenth century. Recently I was going through Thomas Pattenden's Diaries – he was a Freeman of Dover and a local draper who kept a diary recording domestic and local

Camera Obscura

happenings from 1797 until he died in 1819 – when I came across a mention of a camera obscura in an entry for 2nd December 1797. This had been lent to him by a Captain Thorley; he very carefully copied down the measurements and bought a piece of glass for the camera which he intended to make. The camera obscura was used by artists to obtain an image of their subject on a ground-glass screen. Attempts were made with this camera to produce a picture which could be retained and in 1839 the daguerreotype process was invented in France. It seems to have soon crossed the Channel as we find an item in the *Dover Chronicle* of 9th September 1840 which stated that, 'Doctor Simon of Castle Street, Dover, had produced a portrait from life by the daguerreotype process: exposure for eight minutes; sun shining seven minutes in whitish light due to partly concealed sun; silver oxide with mercury vapour on copper plate.' I did in fact make a camera obscura from the dimensions given in the diary, and was able to produce images on printing paper after experiments with exposure.

Amos

One of Dover's early photographers was Mr G.T. Amos, who initially used the daguerreotype method, which I gather he learnt about when in France. He was born in Dover in 1827 and went to sea until he was about 30, first appearing in local directories as a tobacconist at Sandgate about 1856. He arrived in Dover in 1858.

When researching the history of the Dover Borough Police Force I noted in the Watch Committee Minutes of 26th April 1870: 'The Metropolitan Police require photographic "likenesses" of Criminals convicted under the First Schedule of Habitual Criminals Act, on returns made by Gaoler. Tenders to be sent to Photographers for three copies to be supplied.' In the Finance Committee Minutes of 7th November 1870: 'Paid to Mr G.T. Amos 10 shillings.' Later the name of Edward King appears quite often, and then S. Jacobs from 1872 until 1878, when the gaol closed. The latter carried on his trade at 2 Biggin Street only a stone's-throw from the gaol. He had links with Sandgate and showed up there in 1883 when he was a defendant in a court case. G.T. Amos gave evidence as also did A.J. Grossman of Dover.

G.T. Amos had shops in Snargate Street, and when he died in 1914 he was at No. 12. His son Eugene was born in 1872, and carried on the business with his sister Flora after his father's death. He had already made a name for himself with pictures of sailing ships passing through the Dover Straits. He went out in his flat-bottomed dory to get his pictures, and was seen by pilots some miles out in the Channel even in rough weather. He

Beach Street dwelling in 1912 photographed by Amos and Amos

had one of the old mahogany plate cameras, and in inclement weather his coat was draped over it, as he preferred to get wet himself. He was a devout Quaker, and on Sundays he would resist the temptation to go out with his camera if one of the grain ships (a fleet was still operating under sail in the 1930s) passed by in the Channel. The shop was bombed during World War II and most of his material was lost. He died in 1942.

Eugene was a very keen archaeologist, and had recorded many of the various finds in Dover. He had a good number of CLBR (Classis Britannica) tiles associated with the Roman Navy and had more or less pinpointed the position of the Roman Saxon Shore Fort; he would have been thrilled to see what has come to light since. He sent his information to the Kent Archaeological Society and was made an honorary member for his work in this field. Although I must have seen him, I never actually knew him.

Grossman
Alexander J. Grossman, a Hungarian by birth, had a studio at 20 Biggin Street, and was patronised by Prince Arthur during his service with the Rifle Brigade in 1872. This third son of Queen Victoria later became Duke of Connaught and returned to Dover to give his name to Connaught Hall and Park. Mr Grossman took shots of Cannon Street before it was widened in 1895. I have two pictures of that area taken by him with only a minute between them according to St Mary's clock. In the first picture the roadsweeper is blurred, but in the second he is leaning on his broom and, with other bystanders is waiting to be included in the second. Alexander did not waste a lot of time in changing his plates!

Broad and Bowles
W.H. Broad had been at 3, Townwall Street from 1898 to 1909, followed by E. Bowles until 1930.

Dorothy Sherwood and Lambert Weston
Dorothy Sherwood was at 15, Bench Street from 1923 and moved round to Townwall Street. She had links with Lambert Weston, who also had premises in Folkestone. John Farringdon was in business in Maison Dieu Road and later in London Road not so long ago. He worked for Lambert Weston in Bench Street, and told me that his first job in the morning was to swing a large mirror out over the street to catch more light for the studio. He remembered borrowing his mother's pie dish to develop his prints of neighbours' children, charging them a shilling for two prints as a sideline.

Jacolette
Martin Jacolette, whose father was a Swiss miniature painter, appears to have trained with Lambert Weston and became manager until he set up on his own at 1, Priory Hill in or

before 1881. By 1888 he had taken North Brook House, 17 Biggin Street, now occupied by the Halifax. These premises had been the home of a bootmaker, Thomas Holloway, and earlier by an ironmonger. Jacolette had parts rebuilt and his studio at the rear facing north remained until recently. The façade remains except for its modern shopfront. He died in London in 1907 at the age of 57, having made a name for himself as a portrait artist.

50, High Street
G.H. Jarrett was at 50, High Street from 1909 to 1939, when he moved up to Charles Harris's studio at 77, London Road. J.W. Browning was at 50, High Street from 1878 to 1890, followed by G. Bonnaud until 1909.

A friend of mine, Mrs Ridgewell, worked for Mr Jarrett from 1915 until

Martin Jacolette's studio at 17, Biggin Street, now the Halifax Bank

1925, starting at 2/6d. a week rising to 3/-. She recalled for me her job of re-touching prints. The work was done on the glass plate negative, using a very sharp black lead pencil which was sharpened by rubbing on emery paper. Her desk had side screens and a cover to cut out back light and she held the negative over an aperture in the sloping board at the back. The natural light showed through, and she could 'improve' the negative. Head and shoulder portraits needed a lot of attention to remove some of the wrinkles and lines around the mouth for female sitters and the frown marks on the

Jacolette's brochure

men. The proofs were black and white but the finished prints were in sepia. To touch up the print she had a small amount of brown colouring on her thumb-nail, using a fine brush for the necessary corrections. So the camera *can* be made to lie! One day a very irate young man called, after collecting his wedding photographs, and demanded to see the boss. The complaint was that when he was married he had a beard but due to my friend's handiwork this had been removed as she thought it was a shadow. She was told to finish at the end of the week, but when she collected her half crown on Saturday Mr Jarrett told her to turn up again on Monday.

Interior of Jacolette's studio

Harris

Charles S. Harris was at 77, London Road from 1890 to 1938 and recorded some of my early days; many other Dovorians have examples of his handiwork. He made a very good job of the finishing of his prints, and they do not fade. I am told that he had a request to produce a group picture of St. Mary's choir. One of the choristers refused to wear a collar and this would have ruined the effect, but Charlie said, 'Not to worry: he will have one when I have completed the commission!' He often travelled on the trams when I was a conductor and told me that there was one job which he refused; that was to go out in a motor-boat to obtain a picture of a ship on fire in the Channel as he did not want to emulate Mr Amos. In 1936 we were together getting pictures of the launching of the train ferry dock gates at the Crosswall. I had taken a view of the *Hotel de Paris* as a full frontal shot. He suggested that I should take it again showing a side elevation to give it depth. I remembered this injunction when I was taking a picture of Brookland Church on Romney Marsh. I was moving backwards to get the angle right, but fortunately looked over my shoulder as one more step would have seen me wallowing in a dyke.

Whorwell

At 7, Bench Street there was John George Whorwell and his son Arthur from 1891 to 1971. William R. Waters was there in 1867, with Henry Verrall in 1870 at No. 9. Arthur Whorwell recorded some of the events in Dover during World War II, including the cross Channel guns. I have a list of at least 70 photographers in Dover with many of them in Snargate Street readily available to cater for the Armed Forces stationed in the area. Some did not last long and others changed hands.

Amateurs

Some of the so-called amateurs have left evidence of happenings in Dover. When I joined the trams in 1929 I soon came into contact with Harry Elgar, a former inspector. He introduced me to enlarging in his cellar-cum-basement in Tower Hamlets Road. The illumination was a gas jet, similar to a Bunsen burner, and I was launched on do-it-yourself photography. My first enlarger was a biscuit tin, and the condenser lenses were fitted into a Tate & Lyle syrup tin. One of the tram drivers, George Attwood, who died in 1993 aged 93, showed me how to do daylight printing using his outside toilet as a darkroom.

George Archer was another former tramwayman, and we worked together on the East Kent buses. He came along in 1945 to our wedding at St. Andrew's Church with his half-plate camera to record us leaving. Some 20 years after his death I had the chance to turn out his garden shed and found a box full of glass negatives. Some were in good condition in spite of frost and dampness, and among them were pictures of early trams. These I took along to Ray Warner, who was able to get some prints done at Hythe which were later published in a local paper.

Ray Warner

Joe Court of Kent Photos told me that, when he was young, photographers were sent out with only two plates to cover a wedding and both pictures had to be good. How different today where weddings seem to be taken over by the photographer! I well remember that Rosa and I were only allowed two photos at our wedding in 1945 due to film rationing. That was at Lambert Westons, 3 Townwall Street, which Ray Warner joined in 1938 before going into the RAF. He was responsible for obtaining photographs of the damage done by our bombing raids on German cities by flying over the same area the next day.

Archbishop Ramsay at St. Mary's Church by Ray Warner

Ray will always be remembered for his annual Dover Film. For a number of years he took his film to Clarence House to show it to the Queen Mother. I can recall meeting up with him on a number of occasions. Many residents of Dover will recall Mr Taylor's 'Teddy Bears' Picnic' flower bed at Connaught Park. I went up to the park to get some snaps, and straight away Ray offered me the use of his steps to get a better shot. Another memory was going down to the seafront after coming off night-shift, for the arrival of the first hovercraft in 1959. Ray was there, and he told me that there had been a change of plan due to the need to refuel outside the harbour. He asked if I would go round to Shakespeare Beach to tell the BBC cameraman that the craft would come ashore near the Clock Tower. I found him perched up on a platform, surrounded by many car batteries for power, and no earthly chance of moving to the new location. How different it was 30 years later when I joined the BBC team filming the Hoverport for a children's programme. The camera was on the operator's shoulder and the battery was being carried by an assistant.

When I started this story I expressed the fear that portrait photography in the old tradition was on the way out in Dover. Now I am not so sure. Ray Warner has gone, but Eddie Clapson and others are there to carry the torch.

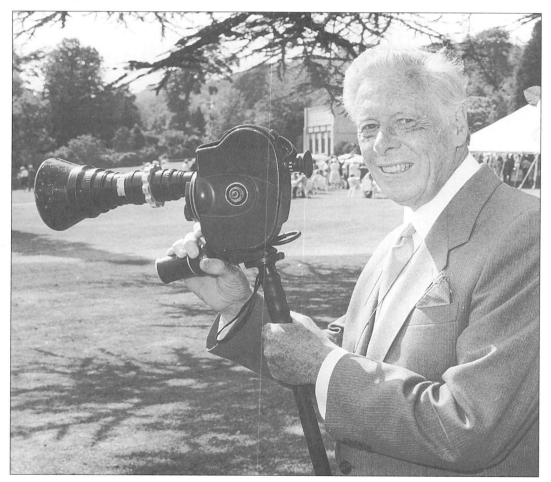

Ray Warner in front of the camera for a change, Kearsney Abbey, 1989

Chapter 13

SHOEMAKERS

Rosa was friendly with the Greenstreet family who had a high class shoemaking business in Dover for many years. In my day most people mended their own shoes – my father did ours and, when he died, my mother took over until I was old enough to do it. Now we have disposable shoes that are never mended! The retirement in about 1990 of Fred Greenstreet, Dover's last boot and shoe maker, led me to do some research on Dover's shoemakers. I went through various records in Dover looking for shoemakers and cordwainers. The latter were makers of shoes, originally in goat leather, from Cordova in Spain. There does not seem to be much information as to the difference between them and it would appear that cordwainers were at the top end of the market. Perhaps this is where the name of 'snobs' for shoe menders came from, but I must be careful not to incur the wrath of the Cordwainers' Company.

Fred Greenstreet in his shop

Luke Howard

Some interesting information appears in the book, *Luke Howard, Shoemaker of Dover*. In the roll of Freemen of Dover Luke Howard's father is listed as a cordwainer When Luke was seven his father died and his mother married a butcher, but Luke was pleased when she managed to get him apprenticed to Edward Goodwin, a shoemaker in the town. In 1642, five weeks after he completed his seven years apprenticeship, he moved to London and attended St. Stephen's Church in Coleman Street, whose vicar was John Goodwin. Perhaps there was a link with his former employer. This John Goodwin was ejected from his living for his radical views in 1645 and Luke joined him when he set up an Independent Church in the same street. They both became part of the Quaker movement under George Fox and later Luke returned to Dover. His son, another Luke, became a Freeman by birth, but was barred from voting at elections as he refused to swear the oath of allegiance. This was overcome later when he made a solemn affirmation after the passing of the 1696 Act which allowed this compromise for Dissenters.

Luke the Elder was one of a number of Quakers who refused to close their workshops on the 25th day of the tenth month, Christmas Day, 1685 (the year started in March at that time). Robert Jacob, Mayor, ordered the shutters of their shops to be nailed shut. Luke, with three others of the same persuasion, were locked up in the Freemen's Prison, known as The Hole, in Townwall Street. He had also been incarcerated in Dover Castle; friends outside the walls had to load food in a basket which was then hauled up by a rope.

Clickers and closers

I searched the five census returns for Dover from 1841 to 1881 for shoemakers and cordwainers and found over 500! Added to this there were about 100 ladies known as

Above: Riding boot 'trees'
Left: Some of Fred Greenstreet's 'lasts'

106

shoebinders, whose job was to sew the soft leather uppers together after they had been cut out by the 'clicker'. The 'boot closer' stitched on the sole with the shoe or boot being fitted round the customer's last ie the wooden model of the customer's foot. The trade seems to have flourished, probably due to the military presence in the area. Later, there seems to have been quite a large export market to officers who had been posted abroad and who had left their lasts in Dover for this purpose. I have seen rows of these on shelves which reminded me of the rows of skulls in Hythe Church ossuary.

Atkins and Gane
In the early 1800s I found the Atkins family. They were Freemen of the town and a branch had become cordwainers. They eventually teamed up with the Ganes and some readers may remember their shop in King Street.

Coulthard and Wilson
Coulthard and Wilson, who still sell shoes in Dover, claim to have started in 1710, but under the name of Robert Low in Last Lane. Early in the 19th century George Coulthard came into the business and later we find

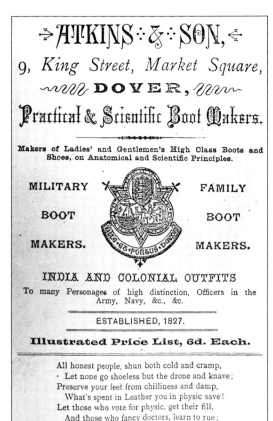

Atkins & Son advertisement

Robert Low's shop in Last Lane in the 18th Century

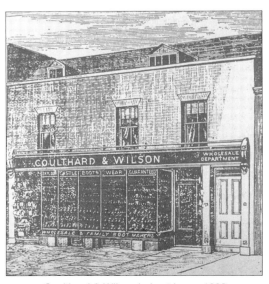

Coulthard & Wilson in Last Lane, 1888

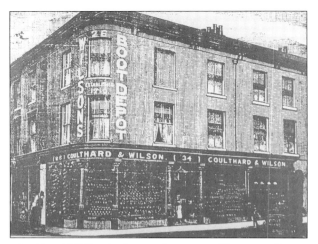

Archibald Wilson as manager. In 1863 a large shop was built on the corner of Pencester Road, but in 1928 it became the Midland Bank when the shoe shop moved along the road. Archibald's sons, Charles and David Wilson, kept the shop in Pencester Road and also the Last Lane premises. I claim some personal interest as my sister joined the firm in 1931 at 2/6d. a week. A small booklet was published in 1888 giving the history of the business and sporting the logo 'Castle Boots'.

Coulthard & Wilson's shop on the corner of Pencester Road until 1928 (now HSBC Bank)

The old shop in Last Lane was destroyed during the Second World War and shoe repairs were carried out in Granville Street. It has been claimed that the Lane was given this name due to shoemakers working there, but there are good grounds for believing that it was really Lass Lane after a public house called *The Lass* in the 18th century; also, old documents list property in Lass Lane.

Woods of Worthington Street

In the course of my research I called in to the Beaney Institute in Canterbury and was shown a copy of a cordwainer's indenture. A Thomas Wood of Chartham had been apprenticed to William Monrow of Canterbury in 1775. This information had come from Bernard, a great grandson whom I had known in Dover. Bernard's father had come to the town about 1899 and had set up business in Worthington Street. Knowing my interest, a friend produced a thermometer which advertised the firm and shows that it was founded in 1782, when Thomas had completed his seven year apprenticeship. The indenture gives instructions to young Thomas not to frequent 'Taverns, Inns and Alehouses, nor absent himself, day or night, and that he shall not play at cards, dice and other unlawful games'. His Master, on the other hand, was bound to instruct him in 'the Art or Mystery or Business of a Cordwainer'.

Adrian Street and St. Crispin

Adrian Street was the home of quite a number of shoemakers and they must have used the St. Crispin Beerhouse in the street. This was the name of their patron saint and it is recorded with its own brewery from 1835 to 1860.

Co-op and Dean's

When I was giving a talk on shoemakers to the Evening Townswomen's Guild and trying to explain how the shoemaker used the heel block for sewing on the soles, a lady interrupted to say that she used to watch her husband doing this and was sure that she still had the equipment. I duly called on Mrs Fincham and was presented with several items. I discovered that her husband had worked in the Co-op shoe repairing department and later at Dean's at the the bottom of Tower Hamlets Road. Dean's had repaired the shoes of the ambulance staff for many years, including mine, so my shoes may have passed through his hands. She explained that it was piece-work at the Co-op with 1¼d. for a pair of heels! If repairs were in short supply there was little take-home pay that week. Her husband did the sewing with pig bristles and waxed thread which used to crack when the stitches were pulled tight.

Cold feet
The old shoemaker preferred to have the chance to make a pair of shoes rather than to repair the machine-made variety. I was told of one old craftsman who was asked by a young lady to make her a decent pair as her feet were always cold. After all his efforts she agreed that her feet were warm, but that the shoes were not fashionable!

Tommy Longley's boots
Most Dover people have heard of Tommy Longley, the landlord of the *Star Inn,* who weighed about forty stones. I have it on good authority that a Mr Becks of Tower Hamlets (Dover) made his oversize boots. Apparently he had one of Tommy's boots alongside his wife's shoe in his shop window to give an idea of the range of his products!

Buckland
At the Buckland end of town we find Assher Kendal who hailed from Fordingbridge, kept the local post office and was also a bootmaker. The census returns show Richard Pay, a shoemaker, who kept the *Chequers Beershop* in Buckland.

John Greenstreet (Fred's father) outside the shop in 18, Bench Street

Greenstreet

All this research started with the ending of the Greenstreet business. This name was associated with boot and shoemaking in Dover for over 160 years. Fred's great-grandfather, who was born in Kingston, apparently went to Canterbury to learn the trade. He then came to Dover and started up in Snargate Street after purchasing his Freedom for £20 in 1827. It was the rule of the old Corporation, before 1836, to insist that you became a Freeman before you could ply your craft. John James, his son, claimed it by apprenticeship to his father in 1848, and John, Fred's father, claimed it by birth in 1877. The firm moved up to 18 Bench Street in 1899 and in more recent years finally moved to 9 Victoria Crescent.

When Fred Greenstreet at last decided to call it a day, he gave me some insights into his craft. I could see that I had a long way to go before I completed my apprenticeship, but I must leave the last word to Fred. When I told him that I was talking to the Dover History Society on the subject he said, 'What do *you* know about shoemaking?'

Fred Greenstreet cutting leather

110

Chapter 14

THE CO-OP

When I was a boy everybody in Dover seemed to use the Co-op shops. We used the one in Cherry Tree Avenue. This impressive building is still standing although no longer a Co-op.

Beginnings in River

The Co-operative movement in the Dover area started in the village of River in 1879. Twelve men, mostly paper-makers, met together in the village school-room to discuss the matter and decided to seek assistance from the Faversham Society, which had been running for five years. One of their Committee members came down and explained how their Society operated, and so the twelve men met again on 11th November and invested one shilling each in the venture. They bought tea, coffee, cocoa and corned beef from Faversham and sold it off to members at a small profit.

By 1880 they had taken over the vacant village shop, fitting it out themselves, and elected Mr Radford

Radford Evans, first Secretary of the River and District Co-operative Society

The first River Co-op shop in 1880 (now Bensted's in Lower Road) with bakehouse at rear

Evans, a paper-worker, as their Secretary. Later they built a bakery at the rear of the shop. This building is now the local newsagent's shop run by Mr H. Bensted and there is still evidence of the bakery ovens at the rear. At first they had difficulty in getting flour due to opposition from local traders; they did manage to get some from Canterbury, but were later forced to obtain it from elsewhere.

Expansion in Dover

They opened a shop at East Cliff but this was in the wrong area, and did not prosper. However, they managed to buy a shop in Market Street with a loan of £400 from the Sheerness Society. By that time they had 207 members and bakery sales had reached £166.15s.3d. a quarter. They next bought a site at River for £2,000 where they built a new store and bakery together with an Assembly Hall. This building is still there and the shop is still trading. The bakery continued until 1930 when a new building was erected downtown. In 1889 they had built a new store in Biggin Street and this was opened on 10th April with great ceremony with the blinds going up, the doors being flung open and the vans coming out of the carriage entrance. That evening 800 sat down to tea in the Town Hall and were entertained by the Town Band playing on the balcony. They were addressed by the President, Mr W. Rayner, and also by Mr Radford Evans their first Secretary, who was by now working as a foreman at a paper mill near Maidstone. He mentioned that when they opened the shop in Market Street the takings were £20 a week and they had now reached £240. Current membership was now 921 and total sales had reached £44,000. By 1898 the membership was 2,105 and the dividend was 2s.2d. in the pound. They had by now opened a shop in Tower Hamlets, an expanding working-class district.

On the Committee was Mr John William Baker who had come down from the North and who had experience of Co-operation in its early days. He was attracted to Kent by work in the coal mines, but had now become a foreman at Mr Herbert Stiff's brickfield in the Tower Hamlets area. Mr Stiff had built the new Town Hall and also the new Central Co-op.

River Co-op bread van with Chitty's flour vans

By 1899 two more stores had opened, namely, Winchelsea, just off the main Folkestone Road, and another in Cherry Tree Avenue. The latter was in the centre of Buckland. I can well remember the store with the cashier up in a little cabin with the overhead money containers shooting across the shop on wires. We took the red order book in, and later collected the brown paper parcel, or had it delivered by horse-drawn van. The Winchelsea shop was very handy as it was next door to the Ambulance Station, where I worked when

River Co-op between the Wars with Common Lane ford in foreground

The Central Co-op in the 1930s

I changed jobs in 1955, and this provided us with sustenance when we had to work overtime.

21ˢᵗ Birthday

In 1901 River Co-op held their twenty-first anniversary celebrations. After a lunch in the Assembly Hall there was a procession of horse-drawn vehicles from the seafront, led by a brake with all their leaders aboard. They proceeded to the Festival Meadow near Kearsney Station where they had sports. The day concluded with a fireworks display and then most of them returned by train to Dover. The 3,000 children present were all given a special mug of which at least one has survived.

The facilities provided for Co-op members in 1901 included clubs for drapery, clothing and coal; the Penny Bank; Library; Reading Room; Women's Guild; Junior and Senior Choirs; Insurance and a Building Society. Many will remember Roly Eckhoff, who was one of those who used to collect for the Mutuality Club which was similar to the Provident schemes. It seems that you had a voucher for £5 or £10 and paid it back on a weekly basis. He was very popular, and his daughter married one of my mates from tramway days. Roly was elected on to the local Town Council and became Mayor, as did Arthur Goodfellow who collected the insurance premiums.

I can remember a plaque on the wall as you went up to the Library and Assembly Hall on which were listed the names of the founder members. I received a letter from Rugby, from a Mr W. Butcher, whose grandfather, Henry Butcher, was a founder member and who later became a baker's roundsman. His son Bill became his vanboy and later graduated to the position of a provision hand at the central store; he appears in the group photo.

'James Simpson' built 1857

Across the road from the central store we had the cake shop with the café above which still bears the date of 1901, but is now the home of the Nationwide Building Society. Next door another shop was added in 1929 selling hardware and electrical goods, and later furnishings. It is now a branch of McDonald's. Later the cake shop was replaced by a Co-op chemist's.

Coal from Newcastle

In 1901 the local Co-op had the use of a brigantine, the *James Simpson,* to bring down cargoes of coal from the North East coast. I have traced it down to the end of 1907 in the Shipping Lists published in the *Dover Express.*

In 1919 170 of the staff had a tour of Kent in six 'Co-operabancs' with lunch at Tunbridge Wells and tea at the Co-op in Maidstone. The Co-op had been quick to capitalise on the demand for charabanc excursions after the First World War.

Co-op outing in the 1920s in a 'Cooperabanc'

Mr. Brown and his bread van in the 1920s

Divi

The bread, for which we purchased a supply of tokens, was delivered in horse-drawn vehicles. We were very fortunate as Mr Brown, the driver, took his lunch-break nearby, and left his van with the horse suitably tethered with nosebag. My roses did very well from the extra 'divi' supplied by the horse power. There used to be long queues on Dividend Days, and the cash collected was usually spent in the stores. In 1930 they built a model dairy, bakery and hall in Maison Dieu Road. The dairy site is now part of the Pioneer (the Co-op's superstore) car park and the Royal Mail has taken over the bakery and hall. At

Co-op advertisement, 1939

about this time they changed the name from River and District Co-operative Society to Dover and District. The hall was well used and I can recall Scout Gang Shows and other events.

Wartime

As far as I can remember the Co-operative buildings did not suffer any great damage during the Second World War and continued to trade throughout. I did not use them as I had by now transferred my custom to Pearks, partly due to convenience and maybe because the girls knew me! I do remember going down into the basement of the central store when caught in shelling. A friend of mine was working in the River Co-op when the war started and wrote on a piece of wood the date of the event and this has recently surfaced after some repairs. This shop had a lucky escape as an unexploded bomb dropped nearby, which defied the bomb disposal experts as it sank further into the river mud. It was eventually retrieved after weeks of painstaking work.

Decline

There were branches in various villages including Aylesham, and after the last war they opened local shops on the Aycliffe and Buckland Estates plus others in Folkestone Road and Elms Vale Road. These, including the butchers' shops, started to close in the seventies. The rise of the supermarkets hit them hard. The Society did make a determined attempt to compete with these large stores by re-housing the grocery department in Biggin Street and calling it Leo's. We still have the Co-operative Funeral Service in the town and the Cooperative supermarket now called Pioneer at Charlton Green but it does not have the feeling of being local and we certainly miss the old Central Store.

Chapter 15

MARKING TIME

Dover Castle clock

I suppose my first interest in clocks dates from childhood days when I visited my grandmother at New Romney. She had a wonderful chiming clock which would repeat when you pulled a cord. My working life seems to have been involved with keeping to time on trams, buses and ambulances.

Dover Castle

It seems right to start my story of local clocks with the Dover Castle Clock, now in the Science Museum. This was found in the keep in 1851 and was initially thought to date from 1348, but is now more or less accepted as being of the 16th century. There is a suggestion that it may have come from the Castle church when it became ruinous. The movement is a verge escapement with Foliot adjustment. Quite a number of these

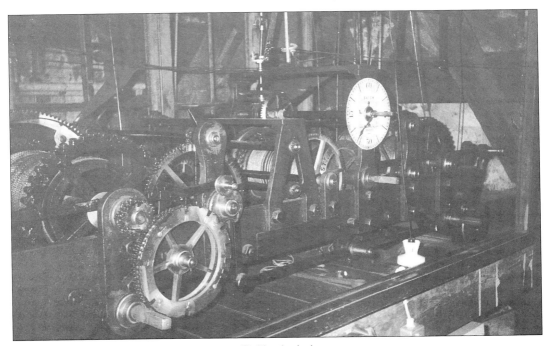

St. Mary's clock

117

St. Mary's hour glass

clocks were converted to the use of pendulums, but it would appear that this clock was out of use during this period and so it survives with this type of movement. Such a clock would only have struck the hours.

St. Mary's

St. Mary the Virgin in Dover has had a clock since 1539, and this appears to have come from the church of St Martin le Grand in the Market Square after the Dissolution of the Monasteries. The present clock dates from 1866 and replaced an earlier clock that was given by Peter Monins in 1733. John Bacon of King Street, Dover, supplied the present clock which cost £208.1s.9d., the sum being mainly raised by public subscription. It was still hand-wound and was well cared for by Tom Manton for many years until

St. Mary's sundial and clock

118

he died recently; now it has an electric winder. On the side of the tower is a sundial placed there in 1676 and which has recently been refurbished. Perhaps this was more reliable than the old clock and could have been used to put the clock right when the sun shone.

St. Mary's also has an hour glass which was used to time sermons. There must have been some groans when the sand ran out and the preacher turned it over to start another hour!

Clock Tower

Most people who have visited Dover remember the Clock Tower on the sea front near the Hoverport. This clock dates from 1830 when the Duke of Wellington was Lord Warden and Chairman of the Harbour Board. Its home was then on the Crosswall. In 1874 the Granville Dock was opened up and it was put in the tower on the seafront. The tower had to be re-sited in 1892 when the Prince of Wales Pier was built. This clock was made by I.P. Paine of London and was repaired in 1881 by John Bacon, a local clocksmith.

Seafront clock tower

Hand-wound clock dated 1830 in the tower

Harbour Station

When the London and Chatham Railway reached Dover in the 1860s they erected a clock tower at the Harbour Station which proved very expensive to them. When I started work on the trams in 1929 it was pointed out to me that it had no dials and this was due to a court case brought by a businessman who lost an important contract when he missed his train up to town. It was accepted that the clock was wrong and to save any further litigation the clock was removed, but the tower remained at least until 1936 and the opening of the train ferry dock. The skippers of the ferries soon realised that the tower was dead in line with the entrance to the dock and so it was truncated and a light put in place to guide them in at night. It is no longer needed as the dock has been filled in.

Harbour Station clock tower

Snargate Street

Snargate Street had a clock erected in 1865 by Mr Igglesden, a watchmaker and jeweller, which was near the old *Dover Express* offices and printing works. It was moved to Deal in 1908 and still survives over a china shop. Thanks to some very helpful volunteers in the Maritime Museum we found a photograph from a 1909 guidebook which showed it in position in the High Street. It is still hand-wound and competes with St. George's clock over the road. There is a strong possibility that at first it was placed on the front of Mr Turk's shop; he was a watch and clockmaker in Deal. The works were in the

Igglesden's clock in Snargate Street

daughter's bedroom and I am told that the apprentices volunteered to wind the clock! Mr Turk's business closed about 1930 and this could be the time when the clock was moved from No.76 to 70-72. Thanks to very ready co-operation from the custodian of the clock I was able to view the mechanism, and I noted that there was a date of restarting in 1931. Perhaps one of the older residents of Deal may put me right.

St. Andrew's School, Buckland
St. Andrew's School at Buckland was endowed with a clock when it was opened in 1858, and kept very good time until the school was closed. The bell, which came from the wreck of the sailing ship *Earl of Eglington* in January 1860, is now in St. Andrew's Church. Sadly, the clock works seem to have disappeared.

Town Hall
The Town Hall has a clock which was placed there in 1883 when the Connaught Hall was built. The clock was supplied by

1883 Town Hall clock

Hand-wound Town Hall clock

E. Dent & Co. of London but John Bacon has his name on part of the gear train. In the Maison Dieu there is a tavern clock made by Emmanuel Levey, a clockmaker from Strond Street, who was in business in 1818. It apparently came from the old Guildhall in the Market Square.

New Bridge

There was a clock at 2, New Bridge which survived the ravages of two world wars and would now be in the middle of the A20 dual carriageway. This was always known as 'Ching's,' being the name of a watchmaker in business there from 1900 onwards. The clock was there when an ornamental archway was erected in 1883 for the visit of the Duke of Connaught. The shop was originally owned by the Woodruff family, who moved there in 1865 from Snargate Street. Miss Harriet Woodruff presented a clock to the town in memory of her brother in 1890 and it still exists below the balcony in the Town Hall.

New Bridge clock

The New Bridge clock was sold about 1960 to Mr Gibbs, who owned the Old Curiosity Shop in Castle Street, and was placed in store, but was to my knowledge never erected. Perhaps some local resident can remember what happened to it. At the moment there is a fairly modern clock over the premises, now a solicitor's.

Cromwell Marsh
Mention must be made of Cromwell Marsh, whose shop was opposite the Town Hall up to the outbreak of World War II. Many will remember the notice in his window showing a very small lad being addressed by his boss, 'Late again! No excuses! I've always told you that Cromwell Marsh will repair your alarm and let you have it back the same day.' I can still see him sitting in the window, working at his bench and keeping an eye on the Town Hall clock above, which I believe he maintained.

Dover College
Dover College has a clock tower, but the clock has been electrified, with a black box which provides an impulse to move the hands, and also to strike the hours. However, the old mechanism still survives and dates from 1892, having been given in memory of the faithful services rendered by Louisa, the wife of the first headmaster.

Buckland and River
Buckland Paper Mill still has a clock which is hand-wound and at one time used to strike the hours, but this was disconnected during the last war for security reasons. Frank Betts took great care of the clock and was pleased to show me its works. There was a clock in the old Tollgate House opposite the *Three Cups* on Crabble Hill which was moved to the shelter in Connaught Park. Kearsney Abbey once had a clock on the old stables and which is still in store at the Dover Museum.

Dover College clock tower

Time signals

We must not forget other reminders of the passing of time. On 2nd June 1859 they began to fire the Noon Gun from the Castle and did so until 1913. It resumed in 1919 and continued until 1923 according to records, but I am sure I remember it in the 1930s. Another time-check came from the various work-places. I have memories of a steam whistle at Buckland Paper Mill. The Packet Yard had, I believe, a bell, but the klaxon at Scott's Dye Works is imprinted on my memory from tramway days. We left the terminus at the Crosswall at 12.28 and hopefully arrived outside the works as the hooter sounded to collect the girls as they left for their dinner break. They were a good crowd and gave us the right fare as it was a rush to collect all the fares before reaching the New Bridge stop.

We were not issued with a watch on the trams, but there was a Bundy time-clock at each terminus and the driver had to insert his key before leaving. Since I retired I don't have to worry so much about time but I still wake at 6 a.m. and get on the move.

Buckland Paper Mill clock tower

Chapter 16

'THE MOST READYEST OF DESPATCHES'

The postal service has always been important to Dover and Dover has always been important to the postal services. Arrangements for sending communications to other countries by the shortest sea route, Dover, could go back to Roman times. We know that a Royal Charter of 1227 conferred on Dover the monopoly of cross-channel traffic.

Dover-Calais packet service
There had been a fairly efficient postal system introduced across the water, and a Dover-Calais packet service had been set up in 1633. The packets had 'letters of protection', which gave them some immunity from attack. There was an attempt to speed-up the mails as the packet boats were being held back by business interests to carry more passengers and cargo. At this time Dover Harbour was shallowing due to shingle and mud, and this meant that shipping had difficulty in leaving at low water. The Clerk of the Passage gave evidence that the mail should be put on board in the Roads outside the harbour. The harbour problem worsened and continued up to the reign of Queen Anne, when a Water Bailiff was appointed to superintend the embarking and disembarking of passengers and mail in the bay.

Post boys
On the Continent they had what was known as the 'staffeto' or a series of stage points. The system was introduced on the Dover Road, starting at Southwark and continuing via Dartford, Rochester, Sittingbourne, Canterbury and Dover. These stages were based on inns with the landlord as postmaster, and responsible for providing the relief horses. The riders were paid a shilling a day, but often these payments were very much in arrears. William Hugessen, who owned the *Greyhound Inn*, was Post Master at Dover, and was prepared to hand the post mastership over to his tenant Edward Whetstone. The latter was prepared to take it on even though Hugessen was owed £400. The post boys were expected to cover seven miles per hour in summer, and five in winter. Edward Ranger was still listed as foot post at Dover in 1649. During the Commonwealth the post masters on the Dover Road were paid, but we have no information as to the arrears of payment.

Farming the mail
The restoration of the monarchy in 1660 heralded an improvement in the postal service. It had been the practice to farm out the mails to individuals who organised the system and made a profit. In the case of Dover it was Lord Arlington and Lord Berkeley who were the original 'farmers' who had a sub-farmer, Colonel Roger Whitley. The 'farmer' that followed was the Duke of York who was Lord Warden of the Cinque Ports and who continued to employ Colonel Whitley. The 'farming' continued until 1711.

First Post Office?
The first record of the setting up of the Post Office in Dover was in May 1663. The Post Master General appointed Mr Jemmett, a member of an old Dover family, as 'Keeper of

Dover's Elizabethan Custom House at The Mount (near today's New Bridge Street)

the Office for Post Office Letters for the Towne and Port of Dover'. There were eight Instructions, the first being to erect a post office, but in 1673 we find that it was housed in the Old Custom House at the top of Snargate Street. Foundations of this building were found during the construction of the new A20 road to the Eastern Docks. Mr Rouse was the Dover Post Master, but the Manager of the Custom House, Mr Houseman, was in charge of the Letter Office. Mr Rouse had to arrange the provision of saddle horses for the six stages needed to convey the mail to and from London. Prior to this foot posts had taken the mail between towns.

Post boys were employed to carry the letters in saddle bags known as portmantles. These were handed over to the masters of the packets for them to tranship the mail to France or Belgium. They found one boatman who was prepared to await the arrival of the post boy for which he was paid £2. The second instruction was that the postmaster was to give his constant attention, and to give the customer the 'most readyest of despatches.' The letters were to be sorted in alphabetical order for both ships and persons, and he was to keep books on the number of letters, and monies received.

It was not until 1784 that the roads were good enough for stage coaches to operate in reasonable safety. In the 1841 Census I found seven post boys and one postillion, who I assume were working on the stage coaches. This was all to change when the railway reached Dover in 1844.

Model of 'King George'

Heyday for sailing packets

The list of packets in 1819 showed 20 sailing ships, and one of these was a very smart sloop of 70 tons, the *King George,* owned by Peter Fector. You can see a model of it in the Dover Museum. Up to 1820 was the heyday of the sailing packets. With more security on the route it encouraged the Dover mariners to improve their ships. These packets became the pride of Europe as they were so speedy and well organised. During this period these swift cutters were built on the Archcliffe Beach. Nothing could beat them, and their fame brought many orders for the local shipyards. We now know that area as Shakespeare Beach, over which the railway from Folkestone travels. These vessels in fine weather left Dover on the flood and the next tide carried them into Calais Harbour.

The wars with the Dutch and French disrupted the service from time to time. In 1697, after the end of hostilities, the Dover-Calais service was resumed, but again stopped in 1702, but Ostend was free from 1706. After the 1713 Treaty of Utrecht the Calais service was restarted, but some Dover packets were operating on the Falmouth-Lisbon route. During the period 1742-1778 some of the Dover boats worked from Harwich. In 1782 there were eight packets, four British and four French, but this ceased during the Napoleonic Wars. No doubt letters were carried over by the smugglers and privateers during this period.

Steam packets

The first steam packet was the *Rob Roy* but the mails were still carried by sail until 1823. In that year the steam-driven *Spitfire* was put on the route by private enterprise, and was adopted by the Post Office to carry the mails. Three more steamers augmented the service,

King Street Post Office 1893-1914

and once or twice a week went to Ostend and Boulogne as well as Calais. In 1837 the Post Office transferred the Dover-Calais Mail Service to the Admiralty, and this continued for 17 years. In 1854 George Churchward had his tender accepted, and in 1863 the London, Chatham and Dover Railway secured the contract for the Dover-Calais route. The mailbags were loaded into nets and transferred by crane to the packets. The Indian mail's journey time was reduced by bringing it down to Dover by rail and transhipping it to Calais and then by train to Marseilles to be picked up by the P&O liner.

Post offices
We know that the post office was transferred to the Strond Street area near Custom House Quay, and before the coming of the railway from Canterbury in 1860 there was Old Post Office Lane nearby, but in the 1841 Census we find it at 120, Snargate Street with William Norwood as postmaster. By 1860 we find it going to a new building at the bottom of Northampton Street. In 1893 it moved up to King Street to a building constructed on the site of the old *Flying Horse Inn*. The next move was to the building in Priory Street which was completed in 1914 by Ellis Brothers of New Romney and Rye. William Ellis of New Romney came to Dover just after the outbreak of war to hand over the building and was making notes, when he, a bearded man, found himself being marched up to the Police Station by an armed escort as a suspected 'spy'.

What happened to all these Post Office buildings?
The Priory Street Office was badly damaged by a shell in 1943 with three of the staff being killed. These premises were repaired and used after the War but were demolished recently, replaced by the new Woolworth building and Dover no longer has a GPO; 120, Snargate Street became a pub, known as *The Old Post Office* and later changed to the *Ordnance*. It was damaged in both World Wars and no longer exists, but No. 110 was a sub post office

Entrance to the Grand Shaft, Methodist Church and Post Office at 110 Snargate Street, during demolition of the opposite side of the road

for many years. The building in Northampton Street became a Sailors' Bethel and was swept away in the widening of Snargate Street in the 1950s. The King Street building is still intact but has been empty for some time.

International mail
In addition to these local post offices Dover has handled foreign mail and packages which is undertaken at their Charlton Green and Maison Dieu Road premises. Currently this operation is threatened with closure. Most of the foreign mail goes by air and mail destined for Europe can be transported by road via the roll-on-roll-off ferries.

Delivery Office
Dover's delivery office is now housed in a modern building in Granville Street but still endeavours to give the customer 'the most readyest of despatches'.

GPO after shell damage in 1943

General Post Office, Priory Street, now Woolworths

Chapter 17

STREET LIGHTING

Oil lamps

While the Dover Paving Commissioners, as a body, dates from 1778, it was not until 1792 that they used the powers that they had to light the town's streets. In that year they called in Mr Wrathall who had been responsible for lighting Canterbury. The first effort was 90 lights with two-spouted oil burners at the cost of £83.6s.0d. for the winter months, sunset to sunrise. In 1794 Mr Wrathall lost the contract to John Bishop and this included the provision to have no lights for three nights before full moon and one night after to save oil and cotton. 1796 shows that John Ruffy of London took over with 140 lamps at 16/- a lamp. Lighting in 1797 was from sunset to midnight, with the night watch on duty for the same period. During the winters of 1798-99 there was no lighting, but in 1800-02 lighting was restored from sunset to sunrise. However by the following year, because of the lack of money, the town streets would be unlit again, but they changed their minds when John Ruffy came up with a plan for four months' lighting at 14/- a lamp. In 1804 Henry Dungey

managed to get the contract at 16/6d. a lamp but Ruffy came back for a number of years with the price of 17/- a lamp. By 1819 Thomas Kent had tendered 15/9d. against Ruffy's 16/- and by 1821 Mr Kent was doing the job at 10/10d. a lamp! These lamps had two spouts with 14 threads and reflectors. The type of fuel used was not mentioned, but could have been whale oil with flat cotton wicks, but again it could have been colza, extracted from crushed rape seeds, which was rather sticky and needed a gravity feed.

Gas arrives

There was a public meeting in 1821 to discuss using gas or 'inflammable air'. A company was formed and by 1823 there were 100 three-jet lights at 35/- a lamp, and 50 Batwings at 68/- a lamp plus the usual number of oil lamps. Batwings were a type of burner which had two jets of gas impinging upon one another which increased the light. Oil lamps must have remained for some time until gas piping was extended. In

Incandescent gas lamp, Pier District, about 1900

November 1829 there was an order to place two oil lamps at the back of the *Hovelling Boat Inn*, which was in the Pier District (Western Docks area). In 1832 the Commissioners of the Pavement ordered that wooden lamp posts be replaced by iron. The *Dover Telegraph* mentions that on the night of 19th January 1849, because there was a fire at the Dover Gas Works, the town was in darkness, and so we can assume that all the oil lamps had gone.

The report of the Superintendent of the Police to the Watch Committee in 1853 is illuminating in more ways than one:

'Great inconvenience was experienced during the five nights of the Full Moon this month of April from the Public Lamps not being lighted, the weather being wet and cloudy, and the darkness consequently great, so that passengers in the streets were coming into contact with each other. The duties of the Police could not be efficiently performed, and the same inconvenience has occurred several times during the past year by the cloudy state of the atmosphere at the time of the Full Moon.'

I have not found any further reference to this attempt to save money on lighting and so it may have produced some result. In February 1885 there was a complaint against PC Richard Carpenter for neglecting his duty in failing to report a lamp out on the morning of the 12th. He was fined 10/-. I believe it was the duty of the police to do this up to the outbreak of war in 1939.

Demolition of Dover Electricity Works, 1938

Electricity

The *Dover Express* reported in its issue of 4th July 1884 that the Town Council was talking about electric lighting in Dover. They had apparently been to the Crystal Palace with members of the Harbour Board in 1882 to witness the advantages of this new form of lighting. In 1884 there were two demonstrations of this in Dover. One enterprising shoe shop owner in Snargate Street lit his premises by this means. He had a dynamo driven by a steam engine at the side of the shop, and it was a good gimmick to attract customers as competition was very strong even in those days. There was also a ball at the Officers' Mess in the grounds of Dover Castle which was illuminated by electricity. The power could have been produced by driving a dynamo with a gas engine. The Council obtained powers in 1888, but failed to use them and in 1893 sold them for about £400 to the

Dover Electricity Supply Company which had the backing of the London Brush Electricity Company.

The story of Dover's electric lighting really started after the building of the generating station on tennis courts near Brook House in 1894. Most of it was demolished in 1938. It was built by Herbert Stiff who had earlier built the Connaught Hall. It is interesting to note that in 1894 they were wiring the hall ready for the new lighting. Arc lights were placed along the sea front and up to the Market Square. One of these was preserved in the old museum, until it was bombed in 1940.

The Company began to make a profit in 1897 after the arrival of the trams. By 1904 the Corporation had bought back the undertaking after obtaining an Act of Parliament. Round about 1906 there were 988 public gas lamps, but only 152 electric, the latter including 64 arc lamps and 88 incandescent.

Electric light outside Maison Dieu about 1900

Lamp standards
In the centre of Pencester Gardens there is a cast iron lamp standard of that time. You can still see the name of the company on its base. It must have been salvaged from another part of the town as this area was a timber yard up to about 1924. Due to their cast iron construction they were vulnerable to attacks by motor vehicles. The one near the Town Hall was demolished by a naval lorry in the First World War, much to the relief of other drivers. There was another on an island in the Market Square over to the left behind the market gardeners' carts. This standard was brought down on 1st January 1937 when the buses took over from the trams. Both of these in the Market Square were erected in about 1903. At one time there was another outside St. Mary's Church in Cannon

Market Square tram standard with light, 1903

Street and this succumbed when a bus skidded on the treacherous wood-block road surface.

Some of the lights were fine pieces of craftsmanship, including the one outside St. Mary's Church which would appear to have been a three-jet burner. The one down at the Pier had a glass and mantle (mantles increased the light considerably) and these were brought in about the time that electric lighting was in the air. There was a very fine light on the top of the central lamp standard in the Market Square. Snargate Street had its lights suspended from decorative ironwork.

Gas lighters

Gas lighting needed the attention of a number of lamplighters, but the number was reduced by the introduction of pilot lights and time clocks. I spoke to a friend whose father and grandfather were both lamplighters for the Gas Company. Grandfather Pilcher was given an easier round as he approached retirement, but he did enjoy a little refreshment. One night the son, who had an adjoining section, noticed that Dad's lights had not been lit, and so he decided to cover up for him. At that time I believe the method was to pull down the lever with a hooked stick to turn on the main supply to the light. Later, the son spotted that some of Father's lights were out again, and on going to investigate he found the old chap gaily proceeding to pull down the lever which put them out again. I wonder what words were exchanged between father and son!

During the 1914-18 War, my father had the job of putting out the sea front lights during air raids. This was a rather hazardous operation without the protection of a tin-hat, especially when the ack-ack shrapnel began to shower down. By 1918 the authorities had imposed a blackout, and rather late in the day had ordered some tin-hats for the police.

If you have walked up to the Castle from the town you might have found some steps near the hair-pin bend on Castle Hill. Here was a gas lamp which the Police insisted should be kept burning. Soldiers returning to the barracks decided it would be in their interests to have the light out while they were saying goodnight to the local lasses. The most agile would shin up the pole and turn off the supply. The police then contacted Fred who shouldered his ladder and walked the one and a half miles from Buckland, but then he had an idea to

Electric light Snargate Street, about 1900

stop this happening. He tightened up the tap to prevent it being moved, but the result was that the determined swains found a stick, smashed the glass and mantle, and so doused the light. In later years when the police had transport they did pick up Fred, ladder and all.

Gas lamps continued alongside the electric for many years and the last, in an alley at Clarendon Street, only gave up the ghost recently when the pipes became blocked by corrosion because there is water present in gas.

Medallion produced in 1908 to celebrate 21 years of the Gasworks Welfare Club

Gas works

Some mention should be made of the gas works, which have now gone,

Gasworks, Trevanion Street

leaving one gas holder. The first was under the cliffs near the present Leisure Centre, with a further extension to the site of the present East Kent Garage. Before the bombing of the garage in March 1941 the offices were the old ones used by the Gas Company which had moved up to Biggin Street. A new gas works was built in Union Road after the coming of the railway in about 1860. The company provided a recreation room in 1887 and I have been shown a medallion produced to commemorate its first 21 years. I believe the staff were presented with these. On the reverse was listed members of the Committee including my grandfather's brother as secretary. His brother, Kingsford, was a stoker at the works, with cousin Henry as carpenter and great grandfather George as time-keeper.

Lights out!
Nowadays we expect a reasonable number of lights to be shining through the night, but a report in the *Dover Express* of 9th May 1924 said that street lights were to be turned off at 11 p.m. At the outbreak of the last War in 1939 there was a mad rush to put out all the street lights on 3rd September and I was able to do my courting in the 'black-out'. It was some time before anyone discovered who my future spouse was. The return of street lighting was delayed until after V.E. Day. There was always the chance of a stray U-Boat in the Channel. However, the *Dover Express* did report that the 'dim out' in coastal areas had been lifted at midnight on 10th May 1945. Later that year, the Ministry of Home Security issued a directive that street lighting could be re-introduced when Double Summer Time finished on 15th July, and the Council agreed that this could be done.

Chapter 18

ANY OLD IRON

I was asked if I knew anything about a Phoenix Iron Foundry associated with a Mr Smyth. This prompted my research in to Dover's iron foundries.

Phoenix Iron Works

Some ironwork had been found at Fort Burgoyne not far from Dover Castle which dates from about 1860. After checking old directories the name of Herbert Stiff emerged, and it indicated that in 1887 he was running the Phoenix Iron Works at 96-100 Snargate Street. About this time a friend lent me an 1864 Yearbook which showed an advert extolling the wares of Ismay Smyth, Ironmongers in King Street. Old trade lists from 1791 onwards show a Thomas Ismay as an ironmonger at the Crosswall (Western Docks area). Early census returns give Thomas Senior and Junior, but in 1861 S.R. Smyth had moved to the Crosswall shop. Further research revealed that Edward Poole (Mayor 1840-42) had a foundry in Snargate Street from 1825 onwards. According to Bavington-Jones, Philip Stiff had taken over this foundry, and had passed it on to his son Herbert. Eventually I found an old gatepost in St. Mary's Churchyard which, after removing accumulated rubbish, displayed, to my delight, 'ISMAY SMYTH & Co. PHOENIX IRON WORKS DOVER'. I

set to work with a wire brush and emery cloth, much to the amusement of passers-by, and succeeded in getting a photograph. The 1861 and 1871 censuses give no clue to the ownership of the foundry, but it would seem reasonable to assume that Ismay Smyth took over from Mr Poole, previous owner of the shop in King Street. The Phoenix Iron Works, near the entrance to the Grand Shaft, gave way to Scott's Dye Works at the turn of the century. Scott's continued until 1965 when the AA Hire Service took over the site which is now a Hoverspeed building.

Philip Stiff

For some years I have been interested in cast-iron lintels, which can be seen on quite a number of houses in town. I was told by a relation that they came from a foundry in Snargate Street, and the following information would indicate a connection with the Stiff family from about 1865-1895. Westmount, now the Adult Education Centre in Folkestone Road, built in 1865 as a private house by Philip Stiff, has this feature. The Paddock, built in 1887, has all the front windows treated in this way. Further along

St. Mary's Churchyard gatepost manufactured by Ismay Smyth, Phoenix Iron Works

Maison Dieu Road past the new Magistrates' Courts we find on the left 'Uniacke', now the offices of Stilwell and Harby, with many of these lintels. I have it on good authority that the house was built by a Mr Stiff and it was here that Herbert died of consumption in 1897 at the age of 48. Philip Stiff was an Alderman but resigned after his son obtained the contract to build the new Town Hall in 1881. At the time of the 1881 census Philip was living in Folkestone Road, and was listed as a builder and contractor employing 94 men and 15 boys. He returned to the Aldermanic Bench and died in 1885 at his house in Priory Gate Road. The *Dover Express* reported that he was responsible for much domestic building in Dover and elsewhere.

Until recently there was a drain channel cover next to the Cherry Tree Inn at Buckland, another in Cowgate Hill and yet another I discovered in Eric Road not far from my home all bearing the name of 'P. Stiff'.

Cast iron window lintels

I have been told that in 1872 he built a section of the rail-link from Sandling Junction which should have reached Folkestone Harbour via Sandgate. Due to strong opposition the line never continued beyond Seabrook Station. Between the two World Wars the East Kent Road Car Co. built a garage across the platforms. After the bombing of the Dover bus garage I took care of Dover's double-deck buses there for nine months.

P. Stiff drain channel cover, Eric Road

Robbins
The 1864 Yearbook also displayed an advert by Mr J. Robbins of Buckland Road (now London Road). This family had been in the business for many years, as in the Chamberlain's Accounts of 1699 we find a payment to James Robbins for Ironwork.

John Wright
John Wright of Cannon Street was an ironmonger who appears to have had a foundry. We find his name stamped on hinges of doors leading from the Maison Dieu into the Connaught Hall. Built by

'Faces of four leopards' bollard manufactured by J. Wright

Herbert Stiff, this hall has cast iron pillars supporting the gallery and roof and these showed signs of the makers on the base. After considerable effort it was only possible to decipher the word 'London'; so, these were not made in the Phoenix Foundry. However, in the pavement outside there is a small cover to a water valve which reads 'P. STIFF', similar to the drain channels, and so Herbert used some of his father's products.

The four leopards' faces

John Wright also made iron posts – bollards – used to bar the way to wheeled traffic. His posts are still standing in parts of the town and were refurbished in recent years by some members of the Dover Society. They are distinguished by their four leopards' faces. Some of us made painful contact with them during the blackout of the Second World War!

Why four leopards? This question led to more research! During the mid-nineteenth century when the Stone Hall of the Maison Dieu was being restored, it was decided to put shields of the Lord Wardens around the walls, which you can still see. I have seen the original designs of these shields. Amongst them was one with the four leopards' faces claimed by 'The Free Barons of the Town and Port of Dover.'

The Dover Corporation bought the Maison Dieu in 1834 and converted part of it into a prison. A wall was built between our present library and the Maison Dieu creating a prison exercise yard. In the wall was a doorway which had a shield over it showing the four leopards' faces and this survived until about 1894. We know that up to 1860 the Town Clerk had been using a seal with the leopards' faces. In a letter dated 1st October 1860, the Town Clerk stated that the Corporation had lapsed into the use of the arms of the Priory. The Prior of St. Martin's Priory (now the site of Dover College) had his own coat of arms which was – the four leopards' faces! This is now incorporated in the Dover College arms. The Priory was dissolved in 1535 and that should have meant the disappearance of its arms, but somehow they survived and were appropriated by the town.

The Town Clerk then asked the College of Arms to produce a device including St. Martin and the Cinque Ports' ship. Despite this the *Dover Express* from its first edition in 1858 had the leopards at the top of its front page until a change of ownership in 1873. *Public Arms* by A.C. Fox Davies, published in 1894, still showed a shield with four leopards' faces for Dover.

The 'four leopards' faces' from A.C. Fox Davies' 'Book of Public Arms'

Two pavement drain covers together in London Road but made at different times, one manufactured by A.L. Thomas and the other by Dover Engineering Works

A.L. Thomas

Anthony Lewis Thomas started a jobbing foundry about 1850 alongside the Dour at Charlton. He was responsible for repairing the hand labour machines at Dover Gaol about this period – the Connaught Hall was built on the site of the gaol. Thomas died in 1878 and I was able to find his resting place in Charlton Cemetery surrounded by some good ironwork probably made in his works. The firm continued as A.L. Thomas & Sons, and in 1902 was made a limited company. About this time they had a branch foundry in Snargate Street between the Old Phoenix works and the Railway Packet Yard. It appears that they took over Hills & Co. Boilermakers, who were mainly concerned with marine engineering.

Dover Engineering Works

In 1908 Walter Emden bought the ordinary shares of the company and put his nephew, Vivian Elkington, in charge of Dover Engineering Works Limited. Vivian often had difficulty finding enough cash to pay the wages each week, and was always out looking for work. By his tenacity he kept going and during the First World War he was responsible for maintaining the two-hundred-strong fleet of the Dover Patrol. When peace returned it was again very difficult to make ends meet. Manhole covers and lamp-posts were their

Dover Engineering Works – stoking the furnaces

main source of business, but there was a demand for stronger and better fitting covers due to the heavier traffic. There was a break-through in 1928 when he and his foreman managed, after experiments, to develop the well-known Gatic Cover. My wife's uncle was at that time courting the cook at Mr Elkington's residence at St. Margaret's. He was sitting in the kitchen when Vivian's mother-in-law entered and asked him, as a blacksmith, if he thought the new Gatic Covers had a future. He assured her that they would be

Manufacturing the Gatic covers

Dover Engineering Works riverside frontage, Charlton Green

a success, as events have proved. This she said was a great relief, as she had just invested some of her money in the project.

The foundry moved to Watford during the Second World War, but Dover Council implored them to return after hostilities had ceased. They agreed to come back if they could use the old foundry off Bridge Street. However, even with improved plant and great efforts they were not able to overcome completely the pollution problem. The type of covers changed, and the firm was involved in large projects for airfields, power stations and oil installations. Eventually the foundry moved away to a more suitable location and the site is now occupied by B&Q and the Pioneer supermarket.

F. Morton & Co.

Dover has some marvellous iron gates which were first erected in 1894 by the Maison Dieu leading to the Turkish and slipper baths. They were made by F. Morton & Co. The name does not appear in any local trade directories and an enquiry to the Science Museum Library has failed to produce any clues. Uncle John Fortune remembers moving these gates in 1924 up to the Isolation Hospital that was in Noah's Ark Road, Tower Hamlets (replaced by the Ark Christian Centre). Over 60 years later they were re-erected within 100 yards of their former home.

Research hazards

There have been unforeseen hazards when trying to get ironwork illustrations. I had spotted a raised nameplate on a cast-iron pillar of an empty shop and was kneeling down to examine it closely when a very kind lady whispered in my ear, 'Have you fallen over, Mister?' I hope I managed to convince her that I was doing some serious historical research!

I had also discovered a manhole cover at the back of Dover Library, and so proceeded to get my picture. I then realised that I was rather close to the ladies' toilet entrance and so had to be rather discreet in getting the focus and exposure right. Hopefully, after reading this, my friends and others will realise what I was attempting to do while scratching away with a wire brush on my bended knee.

I spent some time trying to trace ironmongers in burial records at the Library, but it became a standing joke when I asked for St. Mary's Cemetery records to find some 'Stiffs'!

Iron gates manufactured by F. Morton & Co. in 1894 removed from their Maison Dieu site in 1924 but now reinstated.

Chapter 19

INNS AND ALEHOUSES

It was always said that in Snargate Street there were as many pubs as days in the year. Whilst confined to barracks just before retirement I browsed through the 1900 edition of Pike's Directory for Dover, and a rough check gave about 194 pubs for the old Dover Borough. Going back through our directories further houses were added to my list. Then I started on old newspapers, looking for mentions in police reports, inquests, and granting of licences.

A study of census returns for 1841, 1851, 1861, 1871, also gave much information, and another interesting source was the minutes of the Dover Paving Commissioners from 1788-1841. About this time I made contact with Barry Smith who had published a very interesting book called *The Way* which gave a history of those public houses still surviving in Dover. He had spent many hours tracing the landlords from various sources, and it was possible to give a life to many of the old pubs and inns and also to note changes of names.

My index has grown to more than 500 cards but by taking account of changes in names,

'Kent Arms' 1862-1913

there must have been at least 422 different houses during the last 300 years. In 1545 a list was compiled of 37 inns and public houses in Dover. The addresses were in Biggin Street, St. James's Street and Upwall (Adrian Street).

Pier District

Snargate Street and most of the Pier District is on reclaimed land; the sea came up to the cliffs until about 1600. The Harbour was moved over from the eastern side of the town to the west, and this meant the arrival of inns and taverns around the new harbour. This Western Dock area seems to have had a very high proportion of hostelries and perhaps a ratio of one in four to other houses. Developments over the years, starting with improvements to the harbour, have taken their toll. About 1815 a wet dock was constructed and a number of houses on the harbour edge were demolished, and included in these we know was *Noah's Ark* and *The Britannia*. In the early 1840s the coming of the railway from Folkestone meant an end to a number of houses on the shoreline, and included *The Mulberry Tree Inn*. The rival railway company's line coming through from Canterbury in 1860 destroyed a lot of old property and included a number of inns, among them was the *Packet Boat* and *Shipwrights Arms*. Later, a line linking the two railway lines cut another swathe through the area. Later still, the road viaduct caused the demise of another batch. The *Kent Arms* in Limekiln Street was one of those to go in 1913. Strond Street had a few survivors but these were affected by the 1939-1945 War and the street has now disappeared into the harbour complex.

'Granville,' Limekiln Street

144

'Liberty Inn,' Crabble Hill dating from 1861

Newspaper reports

The Beerhouse Act of 1830 which was intended to reduce drinking, led to the opening of many small alehouses and these increased until about 1870. One such, *The Bonny Cravat*, was the subject of court proceedings two days after opening in 1840 because of noisy customers at 2 a.m. To go back to newspapers I found reference to my great-great-grandfather outside *The Bull* at Buckland in 1835 due to a brawl on Buckland Bridge. He was a witness at an inquest and later I found him in the 1841 census, living very near *The Old Endeavour*. Some of the census enumerators were very helpful in giving the full title of the hostelry, but others were loathe to advertise the house 100 years later, and just listed the inhabitant as a publican. The census return of 1861 gives a section from *The Liberty Inn* by the Crabble Tollgate to Cherry Tree Lane. At first I thought that this might have been an earlier name for the *Gate Inn* which from records starts in 1868. However after a tip-off and a close inspection of a house on the corner of Dodds Lane it was possible to see the name still painted on the wall. Inquest reports in newspapers give valuable information as they were often conducted in the public house. One such in 1841 gave the address of the victim as the *Evening Star* in Biggin Street. The woman had called at the *Royal Exchange*, *The Lifeboat* and *Friend-in-Need* and when brought out of the sea was conveyed to the *Hovelling Boat*. These latter houses were all in the Pier District and in the 1841 census we find Louis Piqui (who gave evidence) at the *Friend-in-Need* in Round Tower Street.

Cause is Altered

The period covered by a particular house can be very useful in research, to identify old photographs and pictures. If a view includes a public house with a sign it might be possible to locate the street or period. The Queen Street area covers the sites of the Roman Forts

145

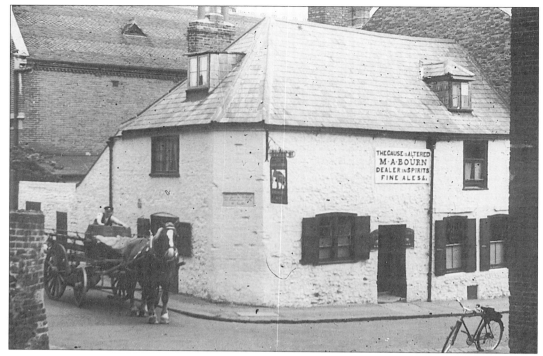
'Cause is Altered,' Queen Street

and there were a number of inns which have disappeared. The *Cause is Altered* at the bottom of Folkestone Road disappeared with the building of the York Street dual carriageway, but it is difficult to be sure of its name before about 1820. Bavington-Jones states that it was the *Black Horse* but this appears to be hearsay, and at that time we know there was another of that name where the *Eagle* (more recently the *Irish Times* now closed) stands. However, there was a *Blacksmiths Arms* in the street prior to the change, and there seems to be some grounds for believing it was the *Carpenters Arms*.

Oldest pub
From time to time the question arises as to which is the oldest pub in Dover. The St. James' Street area seems to be a likely place and the *White Horse* next to the ruined St. James's church is a candidate. It seems that it started about 1760 as the *City of Edinburgh*. There was a *White Horse* in the Market Square in the 17th century. The *Dover Tavern* in Bench Street, formerly *The Guildhall Vaults* and earlier still *The Bull*, is on an old site and is mentioned in 1782. I was still looking for one which kept the same name up to the present day, and in a copy of a *Kent Gazette* of February 1785 I found a notice of a cockfight. This was to be held at the *Cherry Tree Inn* at Buckland, when the gentlemen of Faversham and Ospringe would do battle with the gentlemen of Dover. One can visualise the carriages coming down the turnpike road for this event. The oldest survivor in the Pier District appears to be the *Cinque Ports Arms*, standing in splendid isolation at the end of the viaduct. This was formerly the *Coach and Horses* recorded in 1793 and probably earlier as the building seems to be older. Next door until fairly recently was the *Rose and Crown* dating from 1841 and due to demolition of other property they seemed to lean on each other for support in the best traditions of drinkers!

'White Horse' adjacent to remains of Old St. James's Church and 'pissoir' about 1950

'Cinque Ports Arms' and 'Rose and Crown'

I have also found in St. Mary's Vestry Books about the charity of 'Old Thomas Challice' which was to be paid from his house at the sign of the *Horseshoe* in Biggin Street in 1613. This is noted from time to time, e.g. 13/4d. a year in 1639 and in 1739 it was 10/-. By 1799 the name had changed to the *Saracen's Head* which was sold in 1895 for road widening, and the proceeds were invested to provide an annuity of 9/-. This house stood at the corner of New Street (now Hinds the jewellers) opposite *The Rose* which survived until fairly recently.

On searching through a copy of the *Dover Chronicle* of 1841 I found recorded a song, which had its première at the Dover Theatre in 1799. This introduced the audience to the landlords and landladies of Dover. It was very useful in checking other records. It was sung by Mr Lee Sugg to the tune of The Vicar of Bray. With 16 verses it is too long to quote in full, but here are the first three:

In every age, in every clime
Some fashions had sway, Sirs
And many strange and simple things
By turns have held their day, Sirs
And many jolly things you'll see
In case you turn a Rover
But never jollier fellows meet
Than the Landlords here at Dover.

With famed London City I'll begin
By Steriker now kept Sirs
Then next of note's the Ship Inn
And kept by Wright you know Sirs.
Then Mecrow at the Royal Oak,
The York House Master Payn Sirs
Each loves his friend, each keeps good house,
Each can his bottle drain, Sirs.

At the Antwerp Inn brave Luckett lives,
A noble Volunteer, Sirs,
Who likewise a good larder keeps
With very best of cheer Sirs
At the Saracen's Head lives Henry Marsh
Who once was a Rover,
But now for many years kept,
The Bowling Green at Dover.

Rosa once said that I went to a lot of trouble researching pubs but hardly ever went in any!

Chapter 20

INTERESTS

My interest in history started in childhood. My grandmother lived in New Romney which was steeped in history. She was interested and took me to see the different bits in New Romney. We went up the tower of St. Nicholas Church and she persuaded the caretaker to let me see the Town Hall and Gaol. My grandmother also bought me books like *Saunter through Kent* and *King Arthur and His Knights*. When I got myself a bike I used to ride around Kent visiting all the churches. I went as far as Yalding with a map clipped on my handlebars and a camera.

Before the War, Kent Council for Social Services set up a history committee, the Kent Federation of History Societies, and I was on it from the outset representing Dover. I only managed to get to one meeting because they would hold it on a Friday afternoon in Maidstone. I resigned once but they asked me to stay on to keep the link with Dover. We had a history exhibition at one time before the war in Dover Town Hall.

Many of my other interests were, and are, connected with history or conservation in one way or another. Rosa and I joined the National Trust on Hadrian's Wall during our touring holiday of Scotland and I'm still a member.

Dover History Society
I was one of the founder members of the Dover History Society which also included Lillian Kay and Ivan Green. It was initiated by Miss Kathleen George in 1971 who thought she had better start one when she was asked why an historic town like Dover had no history society. She talked over the idea with Sylvia Corral, wife of the Librarian, contacted some people and the first meetings were held at Charlton Church hall. As well as the monthly

Ivan Green leading a Dover History Society tour of Dover Priory, now Dover College

meetings with speakers, coach outings were organised to places of interest and a weekend was held at Allington Castle. It is still going strong and I am Chairman.

Dover Society and Friends
I was an early member of the Dover Society and have enjoyed their outings and meetings and have contributed several articles. Friends of Dover Museum and Friends of Dover Castle are other interests.

Romney Marsh Research Trust

Members of the Romney Marsh Research Trust on the Union Channel of the Royal Military Canal

As my mother and grandfather were both born on Romney Marsh – my grandmother lived there all her life – I got to know it well, spending holidays there and cycling over its winding roads. It's not surprising then that I belong to the Romney Marsh Research Trust and have joined in its activities including tracing the original course of the River Rother.

Police History Society
I also belong to the Police History Society and over the years have attended several of their national conferences as well as writing articles about the police. If you think that's an unusual society, I also belong to the Brewery History Society as a result of contacting them when I was researching the history of Kingsford's Windmill Brewery. I still haven't researched Dover's breweries but it's on the list of jobs to be done!

Archaeology
I belong to three archaeological societies: the Kent Archaeological Society that I joined about ten years ago and still attend their very interesting meetings as well as going on their arranged holidays – Alsace in 2000; the Centre for Kent Archaeology – as one of the oldest members I was invited to a celebration at Maidstone recently. That all started when I gave £5 to Brian Philp to help get the Roman Painted House project going; and the Industrial Archaeological Society which is centred at Ironbridge. That arose from my trying to find out where the iron gates (now by the Biggin Hall) had come from since I could find no

record of who made them or paid for them. This society told me that a firm in Liverpool made them but I still don't know who paid for them!

Wind and water mills
A visit to Crabble Corn Mill about ten years ago resulted in my joining the Mills Section of the Society for the Protection of Ancient Buildings and I enjoy their meetings and outings. I have been involved with the restoration of Crabble Corn Mill at River which has survived complete with its machinery since it was built in 1812 to help feed the troops fighting Napoleon and is still grinding corn today. I have always been interested in machinery and what with my great grandfather and his father being flour millers, me being born within a short distance of two mills and Rosa working for Chitty's, the flour-millers,

Crabble Corn Mill about 1910 photographed by Buckman
who included his two daughters as he did in most of his photographs

Chitty's Mill

it is not surprising that I have taken a keen interest in wind and water mills. Many of my school pals started work in the Buckland Paper Mill which sadly closed during 2000. That was the last of the six paper mills that used the water of the River Dour over the centuries. I have visited most of the mills in Kent and Sussex as well as some in Suffolk and the West Country. Dover had a tide mill just after the Norman Conquest which was a hazard to ships trying to get into harbour and I have been to the tide mills that still stand at Woodbridge in Suffolk and at Elling at the head of Southampton Water. Years ago I visited Stelling Minnis Windmill when it only had two sails and old Mr Davidson took me up in the cap. I can still hear the grunting and groaning as the great sails turned.

Rosa on Temple Down looking for Burnt Tip Orchids

In the firing line

Rosa and I joined the Kent Wildlife Trust in the 1960s – we got very keen on orchids and were always hunting for them. We found Butterfly Orchids on the old Elham Valley railway line near Peene. I set up my camera but then firing broke out close by and frightened the life out of us – it was close by the Arpinge army firing range! Fortunately we found some more in a quieter spot on the same track near Etchinghill.

Voluntary work

I have talked about my church, scouting, Hospital League of Friends, photography and history interests and have shared with you some of my historical research but I have also been involved in a number of other organisations.

I was on the Road Safety Committee for about five years and had a year as Road Safety Organiser in about 1954.

I was on Dover Trades Council and was its treasurer. I joined the union when I was with the East Kent buses. I had only been on the Trades Council for a few months when Jack Brasier asked me to be treasurer. Well, Rosa was a book-keeper and could always help me out so I did it for five years. The thing was, they had this idea of running a local newspaper. They had raised money from the forty or fifty affiliated unions, but I could see that there wasn't enough money coming in for it. I was supposed to be one of the trustees and I could see the danger that if I signed the forms to be a trustee I was going to be liable for the debts. So I refused to sign the forms and resigned as treasurer. They owed quite a bit of

152

Vi Lane and Rosa paddling at Pett Level, 1964

money in the end which had to be sorted out! Then somebody queried my accounts but didn't ask me to explain. One union would not pay their annual dues until the very last minute – 31st December, but I had to pay out on 1st January so I had to use money from the general funds to pay. Once I got their cheque in I was able to put it right. I stayed on the Trades Council for a while. Then they wanted to buy a typewriter for the secretary and I said they should pay their debts first! It came to a vote but I abstained. Five months later they had to do something about their debts.

I was a first-aider with St. John Ambulance Brigade and also did five years as treasurer of the Dover Branch, but I left in about 1960, joined the Red Cross and became a first-aid instructor. You have to retire officially at 70 and you lose your first-aider qualification but I'm still testing Guides for their badges at 86!

Then I was treasurer of the Ambulance Service social club. They raised money by having a raffle and a dance, but I wasn't happy about the way they were doing it, so I chucked that in. Each time I resigned I had a good reason for doing it. Bob took over and queried my balance sheet – he wanted everything on the other side of the page but eventually found out that I was right!

Walking and cycling

I did have outdoor interests, too, including walking and cycling. By 1941 I had met Rosa and we used to go Youth Hostelling in Devon and the Cotswolds. We arrived in Exeter just after a big air-raid on the city. After our wedding on 17th October 1945 we went on honeymoon to a farm near Ilfracombe. In later years we took our cycles by train to the New Forest and Devon. Rosa loved paddling and took every opportunity. I remember paddling across a stream on Dartmoor. Halfway across Rosa said that it was too cold and I said, 'You might as well go on as go back!'

If you worked for the East Kent Bus Company you were allowed to travel for a quarter of the single fare. Without a car, Rosa and I used to set off at weekends armed with a bus timetable. We had the bright idea of walking round the Kent coast in easy stages. I remember setting out from Margate to Birchington in a south-westerly gale with the sanderlings dodging about on the tide line. Our next stage was to Reculver where we joined in a service in the ruins of the old church – Brian Philp and his 'diggers' were there,

Joe Harman relaxing at Folkestone Warren in the 1950s

too. We did the route in reverse just after the 1953 floods when we had to go through water barefoot in parts. Unfortunately we picked up some tar, but used some butter, left from our lunch, to remove it. In the main street we looked for a café, but when we found one they said they were out of food and were closing. Rosa had half a loaf and some butter, so they cooked us poached egg on toast. We then had the problem of how much to pay!

We covered the stretch from Seasalter to Faversham Creek several times. In 1956 I had a few days owing to me and so we caught the train to Faversham, booked into a little café in West Street and then walked out to Conyer. We returned to the café and chatted to the owners, Mr and Mrs Salmon. He was a County Councillor and he was interested in my activities on the Dover Road Safety Committee. We became firm friends and I'm still in touch with his son, Peter, who was Mayor of Faversham and later of Swale District. When we came home we were greeted with the news of the sudden death of Canon Stanley Cooper, Vicar of St. Mary's.

Another trip was by train to the Isle of Sheppey when we walked along the shore to Warden Point. The going got difficult, so we climbed the bank into a garden which turned out to be a café but it was closed. However, our luck was in. The owner said that there was a joint in the oven and they could easily put some more spuds in the pot; so, we sat in the garden and waited for lunch. We did a similar trip to Gravesend. Looking round for a bed and breakfast place we asked a very friendly old chap for help. He told us to go to his house if we couldn't find anywhere; so, having no luck we called on him. He had lost his wife and was lonely. We were treated to a glass of sherry and Rosa found that they had a mutual friend in Dover. We kept in touch with him until a Christmas card brought news that he had died.

We walked the Royal Military Canal across Romney Marsh and got into trouble with a farmer who was rather angry, but I praised his cows and he calmed down!

When we were walking the Seven Sisters in Sussex and having a rest at Birling Gap, we saw some nuns sitting on the top of the cliffs. So I took a photograph of them and called it 'Five Sisters sitting on Seven Sisters!'

Chapter 21

ROSA AND A FREEMAN OF DOVER

I did not know Rosa before the War, even though she lived up the road and came past on her bike. Rosa lived near St. Radigund's school. Her father was at Salmon and Gluckstein, the tobacconists, which is now a mobile phone shop opposite W.H. Smith in Biggin Street. He was moved to Margate where Rosa was born and then he got back to Dover, took over the Dover shop and lived above it, but he had to retire on ill-health grounds and they moved to St. Radigunds. Rosa joined the Guides at about the same time that I joined the Scouts.

We courted for about five years. I did suggest we married earlier but Rosa said we would wait until the War was over. I had this house in St. Radigund's Road. My sisters had gone. The whole of one wall had been sucked out two inches when the Randolph Road land mine went off and repairs had to be done.

After Rosa left school she went to a shorthand and typing school in Castle Street. Then she went to work at Autocar. One of the things she did when the Granada Cinema opened

Arthur Cloke, Rosa's Father, First World War

Baby Rosa with Mother and Gran, 1917

Charles Chitty's Humber

in the thirties was to take the sixpences in the underground car park which was next to the Granada. Then she went to Vernon Shones – an estate agents in the Market Square – but she didn't get a lot of money there. Dorothy Archibald and Rosa both worked at Vernon Shones. Dorothy went to work for the Admiralty during the War and when Rosa and I were getting married she got in touch with Dorothy who wanted to get back to Dover and arranged for Dorothy to take her job at Chitty's. Rosa left Chitty's Mill when we married but old Charlie Chitty asked her to do his private typing one day a week. He was then eighty something and she carried on doing it until he was 104!

Later, Rosa's father was ill and we said we would hire a car to take him out when I had a week off, but Charlie Chitty said, 'Don't worry, there's my old Humber you can borrow it'. Then he gave it to me taxed and insured. I suddenly arrived at the ambulance station driving a Humber. It was a lovely job and I kept it going for eight years. I had to spend a lot of time on it and in finding second hand parts for it. On one occasion I got into a scrap car to 'rescue' a seat but could not get out – there were no door handles on the inside. Fortunately, Rosa was with me. She climbed up the pile of cars and let me out. It was quite an experience.

Freeman of Dover
I was admitted as a Freeman of Dover in 1989. How did I become a Freeman? By marrying the right girl! The Vicar of St. Mary's visited Rosa in hospital at this time and he said how pleased he was that I had been made a Freeman; Rosa replied, 'Joe wouldn't have got it without marrying me!' She was right. Rosa's father was a Freeman and it is possible to claim it by marriage as long as your wife was born 'free', which Rosa was.

The hereditary freemanship was passed down from father to sons and to daughters for their husbands. Sons could not claim it before they were 21 and if children were born before the father was made a Freeman they were not born 'free' and could not inherit. It was only by chance that Arthur Cloke, my wife's father, knew that he could claim it. His father, Frederick, had died young and it was the arrival of voting papers after Frederick's death that made Arthur curious. 'Your father was a Freeman and had the right to vote in elections,' said his mother. Arthur rounded up his brothers and they all became Freemen.

At one time there were various privileges which were jealously guarded. They included the right to trade in the town and reduced rates for stalls in Dover's market. Freemen received a shilling at elections if they voted and this was soon converted to ale in the local pubs. There was uproar whenever there was an uncontested election and Freemen demanded their shillings regardless!

Apart from hereditary freemanship it used to be possible to buy it for £20 and before 1836 you had to be a Freeman to trade in the town; otherwise you were fined 6/8d. a day. It was cheaper to pay £20 and was one way for the Council to make a bit of money. You could also obtain it by completing an apprenticeship to a Freeman or by having it conferred on you as a worthy citizen by the Common Council.

Joe being admitted as a Freeman of Dover,
28th July 1989 with Paul Watkins,
Dover District Council Chairman

My claim was based upon the Common Council making Thomas Ladd, a shipwright, a Freeman in 1715. Jacob Todd was admitted when he completed his apprenticeship to Luke Ladd (Thomas's descendant) in 1796. Thomas Cloke married Ann, daughter of Jacob, in 1826 and so it was passed down the line.

So, as a Freeman I could have cried 'Fish' on Sundays and grazed my sheep on the sidewalks!

Children
Rosa and I didn't have any children. She was quite shaken during the War and was very edgy and nervous and had a sort of breakdown. Her mother kept on about when we were going to have some children but I didn't like to push her because I was worried that she wouldn't be able to cope, so it never happened. Rosa enjoyed her freedom and we had plenty of contact with children all our lives through the Scouts and Guides and we even 'adopted' the next door neighbours' children!

Rosa's death

I lost Rosa in 1992. Suddenly she started falling about. The specialist examined her and said that all he could do was provide respite care. At one time they took her to Deal. I went to see her and went the wrong way down a one-way street and met a blooming police car! I didn't see the sign. Anyway, I explained that I had just been to see my wife in hospital and they had told me that I had to take her home to die. I wasn't feeling too good. I put her into Poulton's for a week and then Kearsney Manor which I had to pay for. I told Rosa that she would only be there for a week but it was eighteen months. Of course, my bank balance was going down by £250 per week. Rosa died there. She went to the Communion Service in the little chapel; then she was having her lunch, and was gone, just like that.

Rosa's father knew a man who ran a stall in Dreamland at Margate and strangely enough whenever she was taken there she always won a doll. Rosa ended up with about 30 but they had all gone by the time I met her, except for Teddy which she kept to the end of her life. He has now found a new home with Rosa's god child at Taunton. He travelled there by coach in my rucksack.

Rosa, 3 years old, with Teddy that she kept all her life

Chapter 22

FINAL THOUGHTS

I have been all around Britain and parts of Europe and I've enjoyed it but I wouldn't live anywhere else. Of course it's so easy to cross the Channel living in Dover, but not so easy to get to the rest of Britain! Dover is such an interesting town with a lot of history and plenty to delve into. There's always something happening here, too – not always good things mind you! That apart, we do need to think about the future of the town.

The approach to the town from the sea is fine with the great harbour jutting out of the bay between the White Cliffs; the Castle, Pharos and St. Mary-in-Castro on top of the Eastern cliffs; the massive Napoleonic defences on the Western Heights and our attractive seafront. Once you get behind the seafront it's not very attractive these days. Many people regret the Townwall Street underpass, but, on the other hand, without it we would not have found the Bronze Age Boat!

Lots of multi-storied shops in Biggin Street and elsewhere are not occupied above ground level now and look abandoned but in the old days the staff used to live in – above Hatton's for instance. For security reasons, of course, you can't let the flats over the top unless you've got a separate access. We are supposed to be short of places for single people to live. Young people might like flats above the shops in the centre of town; although they might be put off by St. Mary's Church bells waking them up on Sundays!

There are far too many shops for today's needs in Dover's long main street running from Bench Street all the way to Buckland Bridge and many are empty or rundown. Some of the more modern buildings, like those in the Market Square, don't fit in well with their flat

Dover from the sea

roofs etc. – buildings more in keeping would be better. Canterbury is doing away with all its 1960s developments – why can't Dover? Burlington House is another eyesore – every town had to have its tower office block in the '60s but now they are eyesores. At long last they are planning the redevelopment of the St. James's area much of which has been derelict for many years.

Somebody ought to do something about developing the town for the future as we only have the port now as a major employer. We need more local industry. We still get lots of foreign visitors and we need speciality shops to attract them.

The best times
Compiling this book made me think about what was the best part of my life. My time on the trams was a happy one. We didn't get much money but we had some fun. We all stuck together and there was a good spirit. During the Second War there was a community spirit and everybody helped each other and you got to know everybody. After the War I got fed up with the buses – people made sure I didn't get anywhere and so I left. The ambulance service was not so good – not such happy days, especially when I got promoted. Some people were jealous about it, but they couldn't have done the job anyway! Probably the best times were at the Guides' Cottage at Elms Vale during the War with all the gang, producing the Cottage Bulletin and, of course, meeting Rosa there and courting her.

Joe at 86

ACKNOWLEDGEMENTS

We wish to thank the following for their help:

Ashford Library

Anthony Belsey

H. Bensted

Frank Betts

Derek Brown

Buckland Paper Mill

Albert Butcher

D. Button

Eddie Clapson

Cordwainers Technical College

Sylvia Corrall

C.P. Davies

Deal Maritime Museum

Dover Express

Dover Film Society

Dover Harbour Board

Dover Library

Dover Museum

Dover Town Hall staff

R. Filmer

John Gilham

The late Stan Gaskill

Godfrey Gray

The late Maurice Hobday

Bob Hollingsbee

The late Colin Jervis

May Jones for proof reading

Kent Messenger

Susan Lees

Maidstone & District and East
Kent Bus Club

The late Tom Manton

Wally Pascall

F. Pilcher

The late Archbishop Ramsey

The late Edith Relton (née
Greenstreet)

E. Roony

The late John Roy

Science Museum

Lorraine Sencicle

Barry Smith

Denis Stubbs

A.F. Taylor

The late Ray Warner

Douglas Welby

The late F.A.J. Woodworth

We wish to thank the following for permission to reproduce photographs :

Adscene

Eddie Clapson

Crabwell Publications

Dover Express

Richard Filmer

John Gilham

Bob Hollingsbee

Dover Library

Dover Museum

Kent Messenger

LIST OF ILLUSTRATIONS

BIBLIOGRAPHY

The Policeman's Lot *by Mervyn Mitton*
Perambulation of Dover *by J. Bavington-Jones*
These Were My Children *by J. Melhuish*
Buckland 1852-1952 *by Miss O.M. Rookwood*
Dover Buckland Anglo-Saxon Cemetery 1987 *by Vera I. Evison*
Wartime Dover its Post Office and Staff *by A.W.B. Mowbray MBE*
Annals of Dover *by J. Bavington-Jones*
English Provincial Posts *by Brian Austin*
Banking on Dover *by Lorraine Sencicle*
History of Dover Harbour *by Alex Hasenson*
Luke Howard, Shoemaker of Dover *published by the Society of Friends*
The records of William Knocker (late 18th century Mayor of Dover)